Aerospike: Up and Running
*Developing on a Modern Operational Database
for Globally Distributed Apps*

*V. Srinivasan, Tim Faulkes, Albert Autin,
and Paige Roberts*

Aerospike: Up and Running

by V. Srinivasan, Tim Faulkes, Albert Autin, and Paige Roberts

Copyright © 2025 O'Reilly Media, Inc. All rights reserved.

Published by O'Reilly Media, Inc., 1005 Gravenstein Highway North, Sebastopol, CA 95472.

O'Reilly books may be purchased for educational, business, or sales promotional use. Online editions are also available for most titles (*http://oreilly.com*). For more information, contact our corporate/institutional sales department: 800-998-9938 or *corporate@oreilly.com*.

Acquisition Editor: Andy Kwan	**Indexer:** Sue Klefstad
Development Editor: Gary O'Brien	**Interior Designer:** David Futato
Production Editor: Aleeya Rahman	**Cover Designer:** Karen Montgomery
Copyeditor: Charles Roumeliotis	**Illustrator:** Kate Dullea
Proofreader: Krsta Technology Solutions	

October 2024:   First Edition

Revision History for the First Edition

2024-10-15:   First Release

See *http://oreilly.com/catalog/errata.csp?isbn=9781098155605* for release details.

978-1-098-15560-5

[LSI]

Table of Contents

Preface

The last decade has seen the rise of many new database technologies to address the needs of the internet and mobile applications that have become ubiquitous. These systems were built to satisfy consumers whose behavior has changed drastically, as they now expect real-time services from every enterprise with which they are interacting. As a result, there has been a huge increase in the number of new database technologies invented to help make this happen.

In this book, we present a modern, high-performance distributed database system that has all of the important features of traditional database systems like strong consistency, durability, and availability while also providing real-time distributed transactional and query capabilities at scale for a wide variety of real-time applications that previous generations of technologies could not satisfactorily handle.

The people who will benefit from this book are those who want to learn how to rapidly develop real-time applications in the service of millions of consumers and quickly ramp up to internet scale. Developing such applications on Aerospike lets you analyze more data in real time to make better decisions within strict, time-bound service-level agreements (SLAs). Aerospike enables you to minimize your per-transaction costs by leveraging the latest in hardware and cloud infrastructure. It increases availability by using synchronous and asynchronous replication mechanisms, preserving strong consistency while maximizing availability and minimizing replication costs. And it handles multiple data models on the same database platform. All of this adds up to an opportunity to create powerful new applications.

Conventions Used in This Book

The following typographical conventions are used in this book:

Italic
> Indicates new terms, URLs, email addresses, filenames, and file extensions.

Constant width

> Used for program listings, as well as within paragraphs to refer to program elements such as variable or function names, databases, data types, environment variables, statements, and keywords.

Constant width bold

> Shows commands or other text that should be typed literally by the user.

Constant width italic

> Shows text that should be replaced with user-supplied values or by values determined by context.

 This element signifies a tip or suggestion.

 This element signifies a general note.

 This element indicates a warning or caution.

O'Reilly Online Learning

 For more than 40 years, *O'Reilly Media* has provided technology and business training, knowledge, and insight to help companies succeed.

Our unique network of experts and innovators share their knowledge and expertise through books, articles, and our online learning platform. O'Reilly's online learning platform gives you on-demand access to live training courses, in-depth learning paths, interactive coding environments, and a vast collection of text and video from O'Reilly and 200+ other publishers. For more information, visit *https://oreilly.com*.

How to Contact Us

Please address comments and questions concerning this book to the publisher:

O'Reilly Media, Inc.
1005 Gravenstein Highway North
Sebastopol, CA 95472
800-889-8969 (in the United States or Canada)
707-827-7019 (international or local)
707-829-0104 (fax)
support@oreilly.com
https://oreilly.com/about/contact.html

We have a web page for this book, where we list errata, examples, and any additional information. You can access this page at *https://oreil.ly/aerospike*.

For news and information about our books and courses, visit *https://oreilly.com*.

Find us on LinkedIn: *https://linkedin.com/company/oreilly-media*.

Watch us on YouTube: *https://youtube.com/oreillymedia*.

Acknowledgments

We've had a great time working on this book together and, as a group, we would like to first thank our fellow authors. A group project like this can be great or awful entirely depending on who you're doing it with. Having four people from three different companies that got along famously and all pulled in the same direction made the project far more enjoyable and the end result a better book. We'd also like to express our gratitude to all of the tech reviewers, especially Ido Barkan and Peter Milne, who really dove into the details and gave us useful feedback. Most of all, we'd all like to thank Gary O'Brien, our infinitely patient O'Reilly editor, who shepherded us through this project in the best tradition of cat herders everywhere. Without his help and encouragement, this project would probably still be in progress.

V. Srinivasan

> For the past 15 years, the work at Aerospike has been my singular focus and it would have been impossible for me to do this without the help I received from countless people both within and outside Aerospike, especially my wife, Viji. I'd like to thank my cofounder, Brian Bulkowski, who invited me to join him in this project in 2009. While it is impractical to list everyone who has contributed to Aerospike, I'd like to specially recognize Andrew Gooding and Sunil Sayyaparaju for their brilliant technical contributions that have largely shaped Aerospike into the product that it is today.

Tim Faulkes

There are so many people to thank who helped make this book a reality. My wife, Jordan, who encouraged me and put up with the long hours needed to write this. Piyush Gupta for keeping me honest on technical details and discussing some of the data modeling techniques with me. Evan Cummack and Matt Bushell for reviewing chapters and discussing the structure of the book. The whole engineering team at Aerospike for creating an awesome, robust product with special shout-outs to Brian Nichols, Andrew Gooding, and Kevin Porter. And, of course, the O'Reilly team, especially Gary O'Brien and Andy Kwan.

Albert Autin

To my wife, Karamia, thank you for your support throughout this adventure. Together, we've pursued our dreams, even when they've taken us in unexpected directions.

To my brother, Jerome, and his wife, Lauren, thank you for your sacrifices and guiding me through my formative years. I'll always look back fondly on our nights spent playing Shostakovich and The Cure, cooking quiche and pot pies, and leaping into Barton Springs.

Thanks to Tim Faulkes for educating me on the deeper aspects of Aerospike back in 2015, Meher Tendjoukian for your assistance during those long support calls, and Andrew Gooding for patiently listening to my untenable ideas. My gratitude extends to the entire Aerospike team for their remarkable product, support, and vision.

Paige Roberts

Thanks to Jess Haberman, my first O'Reilly editor, who gave me confidence that I could do this technical book writing thing. And many thanks to my husband Joe for putting up with me spending tons of time plinking away on a keyboard and ignoring him. I learned so much from Gary and the writing team. It's been a privilege.

## CHAPTER 1

Introduction to Aerospike

Aerospike is a distributed NoSQL database with exceptional speed on both reads and writes and a strong uptime percentage. This sounds reasonable and normal for a database, but it doesn't put into perspective the capabilities of this software.

In the data management industry, we have certain limitations in our minds as to what a database can do. Aerospike doesn't live by those restrictions. Submillisecond transaction speeds are normal, even on petabyte-scale data volumes, without resorting to huge clusters. This is not what any sensible, experienced data analyst or database administrator expects. To truly understand and get what you want most out of Aerospike, you'll have to set aside a certain amount of what you "know" and come at this with an open mind.

NoSQL databases have traditionally achieved high performance and scale by relaxing consistency guarantees. However, this trade-off is a poor choice for use cases that require a high level of data correctness. A majority of applications contain some data requiring correctness and consistency, such as financial data, as well as data that can tolerate limited consistency violations, such as data from clickstreams.

Aerospike maintains strong consistency along with high-performance characteristics that have been proven in hundreds of mission-critical production deployments with several years of continuous uptime in the face of typical hardware and network failures. The type of strong consistency that Aerospike implements can satisfy the stringent requirements needed for applications that are dependent on a system of record. Aerospike achieves its high performance on less hardware by making optimal use of flash storage, utilizing vertical scaling to effectively use the hardware on each server instance, and achieving excellent horizontal scaling using distributed clustering algorithms.

For the rest of this book, we'll assume you have a good working knowledge of data, databases, and how to work with them. The book will focus on what makes Aerospike unique, and what you need to know about how it differs from other databases so that you can get the most out of it.

What Makes Aerospike Different

Strong consistency can be fast, even at scale.

While there are many important differences between Aerospike and other databases, the combination of strong consistency and high speed regardless of data scale is the essence of what makes Aerospike unique. And thanks to its ability to take advantage of flash storage devices, it does this on relatively small clusters.

First, consider Aerospike's speed with consistency. A widespread view maintains that there will always be a major performance gap between running a system with relaxed consistency and one that supports strong consistency.

You've likely heard of Brewer's CAP theorem (consistency, availability, and partition tolerance) (*https://oreil.ly/q0B1X*). It has been one of the founding principles of NoSQL systems, yet Aerospike has spent over a decade pushing the envelope in this area with remarkable results.

Some Aerospike use cases require strong consistency without losing the system's high performance capabilities. Aerospike's unique strong consistency algorithm can achieve this, maintaining high performance and low latency while maximizing system availability.

The requirements Aerospike meets in order to accomplish this are:

- Not losing writes under any circumstances, including during split-brain scenarios and other situations where multiple nodes are missing from the cluster
- Avoiding stale reads
- Both adding and removing capacity (nodes) through simple operational procedures that do not result in consistency or availability breaches
- Allowing developers and system architects to choose strong consistency or higher availability on a per-dataset basis
- Maintaining both availability and consistency during a rolling software upgrade process provided the number of nodes down at any time is fewer than the replication factor of the data

Availability and Consistency (AP and CP Modes)

Partition tolerance must always be prioritized in any cluster distributed system. Aerospike enables you to configure which is the most important to your particular use case, availability or consistency, AP (availability, partition tolerance) mode or CP (consistency, partition tolerance) mode.

Many distributed databases sacrifice consistency, dropping to a state known as *eventual consistency*, where data across a cluster will eventually reach a state where the data is the same on all nodes of the cluster, but there will be a period of time when this is not the case.

Transactional databases, however, generally require the opposite of eventual consistency—in other words, strong consistency. In these databases, any node can be queried and produce an identical result.

Regardless of which you choose to prioritize, consistency or availability, Aerospike works to maximize the other as well.

Availability first (AP Mode)

Even when configured to prioritize availability, in AP mode, violating consistency is rare in a properly running Aerospike system. In Chapter 5, you'll learn more about the two conditions that might cause consistency to be affected in AP mode.

Consistency first (CP Mode)

While AP mode provides a surprisingly high level of data consistency, it isn't perfect. When data correctness is essential, choose CP mode, prioritizing consistency over availability. Most systems that provide strong consistency require a minimum of three copies.[1] So, if a cluster splits, one of the two subparts of the cluster can allow writes if it has a majority of (two out of three) copies of a data partition.

Aerospike optimizes cluster size by allowing storage of only two copies. Using an adaptive scheme that adds more write copies on the fly in situations where they are necessary, Aerospike provides the theoretically correct result of a three-copy distributed system while only paying the infrastructure and processing costs for keeping two copies of the data.

Chapter 5 discusses the few conditions when availability is impaired in CP mode, as well as other important aspects of the basic architecture of Aerospike. Chapter 9 dives even deeper into how this is accomplished.

---

1 Leslie Lamport, *Lower Bounds for Asynchronous Consensus*. Microsoft Research, Microsoft Corporation, MSR-TR-2004-72 (2006).

Flash Optimization

Another key difference between Aerospike and other databases, which allows it to operate at in-memory database speeds while using around one-tenth the number of cluster nodes, is its ability to take advantage of the characteristics of flash storage in its hybrid storage approach.

Besides throughput and latency characteristics, the ability of a database is characterized by the amount of data that can be stored and processed. Leveraging flash requires a different storage mechanism from the standard spinning disks that most databases use. Aerospike software is designed to take advantage of those differences.

Flash storage (SSDs) can be a game changer for real-time data. While in-memory configurations, which use computer memory for all data storage and computations, can be somewhat faster, Aerospike has demonstrated that SSDs can increase the per-node capacity between 10 and 100 times, often with little perceptible loss of performance.

An Aerospike system that uses flash storage can manage dozens of terabytes of data on a single machine with submillisecond record access (read and write) times. This design is possible because the read latency characteristic of input and output (I/O) in SSDs is predictably fast, regardless of whether it is random or sequential. At the time of writing, a typical commodity server can be affordably set up with 30 TB of high-performance flash and 1 TB of memory—providing 30 times the capacity of a 1 TB in-memory database on the same server.

Aerospike supports multiple kinds of storage architectures: *hybrid flash* (aka *hybrid memory*), *in-memory*, and *all-flash*. To leverage flash storage, Aerospike implements a hybrid model where data resides in flash storage, and indexes reside entirely in memory. Figure 1-1 illustrates the hybrid and in-memory architectures side by side.

One interesting thing you'll notice in Figure 1-1 is that two namespaces in Aerospike can be configured differently, one to use only memory, and the other to use a hybrid of memory and flash. They can coexist in the same node without issue. Both namespaces have their primary key index in memory. The main difference is that the in-memory namespace also stores its data in memory. The hybrid namespace uses a slightly more involved process to save its data to flash storage. Chapter 5 will describe this process in more depth.

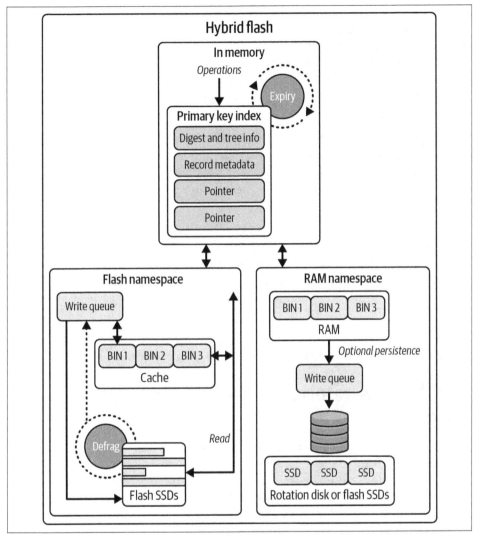

Figure 1-1. Hybrid flash and in-memory architectures

Since storage I/O is the slowest point in any application that uses a storage device, storage I/O is not required to traverse the index, even when data is stored on flash devices. This makes read performance in Aerospike high and predictable. This design is possible because the read latency characteristic of I/O in NAND flash (the type of flash drive most commonly used in servers) has little penalty for random access. Database access first traverses the index and acquires metadata that indicates where the required data is located. If the data element is located in a local cache, it can be returned without I/O access at all. If it is in flash storage, a single I/O will be executed to bring the entire element into local memory.

This ability to do random read I/O comes at the cost of a limited number of write cycles on SSDs. In order to avoid creating uneven wear on a single part of the SSD, and to colocate all the data of a record in one location, Aerospike does not perform in-place updates. Instead, it employs a copy-on-write mechanism using large block writes. This wears the SSD down evenly, improving device durability, and guarantees that all data for a particular record is in one location, thus preventing fragmentation of data in storage.

Gathering writes together into large blocks enables very high write throughput by combining hundreds of transactional writes into a single large block write and ensures that the internal coalescing algorithms inside a flash controller do less work. The copy-on-write mechanism is also beneficial for data correctness and recovery in case of hardware failures.

Aerospike is typically configured to bypass the operating system's filesystem and instead uses attached flash devices directly as a block device using a custom data layout. This avoids the problem of depending on filesystems that are not optimized for flash. Unoptimized filesystems would generate extra I/O and wear as well as complexity in matching an operating system's data commit policy to the filesystem's.

These techniques are instrumental in providing Aerospike the unique ability to support extremely high application write rates in production while maintaining in-memory-class read response times, as well as high data correctness.

What Makes Aerospike Optimal for Submillisecond Workloads

Beyond its unique high consistency and availability, and its small cluster sizes for demanding workloads at scale, the architecture of Aerospike is focused on read latencies lower than a millisecond on any volume of data, even with extreme throughput levels. You might expect this level of performance to require massive clusters of hardware or cloud instances, but thanks to its flash utilization and other optimizations, Aerospike frequently accomplishes this goal with a tenth (or fewer) the number of nodes compared to similar purely in-memory databases. Several aspects of the Aerospike architecture make this possible, including a shared-nothing architecture, the ability to maintain predictable high performance levels with high availability, and making optimal use of each node in a cluster.

Avoiding Hotspots with Shared-Nothing Architecture

All servers in an Aerospike cluster are peers, with no master, leader, or other differentiated nodes. For horizontal scaling, Aerospike uses a shared-nothing architecture in which all nodes forming the database cluster are homogeneous—identical in terms of CPU, memory, storage, and networking capacity. A key component of this scheme is a uniform data partitioning algorithm that eliminates all skew in terms of data distribution across database cluster nodes, thereby ensuring there are no hotspots.

Access to flash storage is done in a massively parallel manner, creating a transparent data layout similar to a high-performance "RAID-0" striping system. The keys are mapped into various devices within nodes in a uniform manner. This ensures that an even amount of data is stored on every node and every flash device, thus making sure that all hardware is used equally and the load on all servers and storage devices is balanced.

These strategies and several more you'll learn about later prevent "hot spots" and require no configuration changes even as the workload changes. For example, in Figure 1-2, you can see 80-way parallelism illustrated in a cluster of 16 nodes with 5 flash devices on each node.

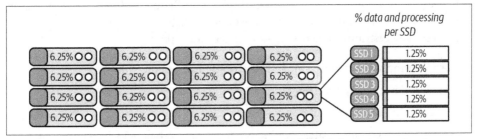

Figure 1-2. Massively parallel data access on a 16-node hybrid flash Aerospike cluster showing data and processing load per node

Keeping Performance Predictable with Resilient Stability

There are multiple things that make Aerospike's performance predictable and consistent. You just learned that storage device I/O is not required to access the index in hybrid-memory or in-memory configurations. For accessing data, the previous section mentioned that the read latency for random access to SSDs is predictably low, and skipping the operating system layer makes every piece of data exactly one I/O hop to retrieve, regardless of whether it is random or sequential. Beyond that, several architectural features keep the cluster as stable and self-healing as possible so performance remains relatively constant over time.

An automatic partitioning of the key space and an automatic data rebalancing mechanism ensures that the transaction volume is distributed evenly across all nodes and is robust in the event of any node failures happening during the rebalancing process itself. The system is designed to be continuously available, so data rebalancing doesn't impact cluster behavior.

By not requiring operator intervention, clusters will self-heal even at demanding times. You can configure and provision your hardware capacity and set up replication/synchronization policies so that the database recovers from failures without affecting users, and you can sleep at night.

The mapping from partition to node (partition map) is exchanged and cached with the clients. Sharing of the partition map with the client is critical in making client-server interactions extremely efficient. This is why, in Aerospike, access to data from the client requires a single network request to the server node containing the data item and a maximum of one storage I/O operation each time. In steady state, the scale-out ability of the Aerospike cluster is *purely* a function of the number of clients and server nodes. This guarantees the linear scalability of the system as long as other parts of the system—like network interconnect—can absorb the load.

To avoid hotspots that could affect performance, Aerospike colocates indexes and data to avoid any cross-node traffic when running read operations or queries. Writes may require communication between multiple nodes based on the replication factor. Colocation of index and data and a robust data distribution hash function give you nice, even data distribution across nodes. This ensures that:

- Application workload is uniformly distributed across the cluster.
- Performance of database operations is predictable.
- Scaling the cluster up and down is easy.
- Live cluster reconfiguration and subsequent data rebalancing is simple, nondisruptive, and efficient.

Reducing Cluster Size with Optimal Use of Each Node

For a system to operate at extremely high throughput with low latency, it is necessary not just to scale out across nodes but also to scale up "(vertically)" on each node. This section discusses system-level details that help Aerospike scale up to millions of transactions per second at submillisecond latencies. The techniques used by Aerospike apply to any data storage system.

The ability to scale vertically on each node effectively means the following:

- Higher throughput levels on fewer nodes.
- Better failure characteristics, since probability of a node failure typically increases as the number of nodes in a cluster increases.
- Easier operational footprint. Managing a 10-node cluster versus a 200-node cluster is a huge win for operators.
- Lower total cost of ownership. This is especially true once you factor in SSD-based scaling.

The basic philosophy here is to enable the system to take full advantage of the hardware by leveraging it in the best way possible. To accomplish this, Aerospike is written in the C language and has a number of CPU and network optimizations that allow it to handle millions of single-record transactions per second with sub-millisecond latencies on a single node.

The scale-up architecture can typically reduce the cost of ownership of a system using the hybrid memory configuration by up to 80% compared to the same system using a pure in-memory configuration. The surprising part is that no compromise is needed in application-level performance to get the savings in infrastructure and operational costs. See Chapter 5 for more information about the architecture that makes this possible.

Why Milliseconds Matter

For many workloads, Aerospike would have a ridiculously overpowered level of performance, like using a Formula 1 race car for your daily commute. However, for some use cases this level of speed isn't just nice to have, it's essential. Whether the scale of data is fairly small or extremely large, the key factor for success is often performance. For a variety of industries, particularly the more modern industries built on the speed expectations of digital natives, milliseconds matter as operations have to be executed within strict time-bound service-level agreements (SLAs).

Some examples:

- The ad-tech industry has to handle millions of ad auctions per second, each within a bidding loop of 100 milliseconds. Too slow and no bid wins: the audience has clicked to a different window and the ad is never displayed.

- As a video game is played, in-game personalized optimizations can mean the difference between success for the game and the gaming company and a game that flops.

- For real-time events (ticket purchases for popular events, fantasy sports where millions of players are finalizing their teams in the final minutes before a match starts, etc.) the ability to handle enormous load spikes, up to 100× more than normal load, can make the difference between success and failure of a billion-dollar business.

- For financial companies with digital payment options, detecting fraud within the transaction execution time itself (i.e., within 200 milliseconds) can mean the difference between normal customer service and big problems like financial loss, regulatory exposure, etc. With the right level of speed, fraud detection becomes fraud prevention, but only if the system can handle both the volume and the speed needed.

There are many industries where people do not yet see the need for submillisecond response times simply because they find it hard to conceive of such rapid access to their data. Faster data access can result in business changes that have considerable potential to increase top-line revenue.

Consider a trading company that runs compliance algorithms in a nightly batch on the mainframe, potentially missing noncompliant trades during the day. Faster data access could mean those compliance algorithms could be run every few minutes, eliminating this risk.

Or consider that a digital identity management company could accurately verify the identity of a user three times faster with a higher level of confidence by using more data in real time to make more accurate decisions.

Chapter 10 discusses some in-depth examples of use cases that are ideal for Aerospike's strengths.

Summary

In this book, you'll learn the basics of how to go from being an Aerospike beginner to having the confidence to use it daily. You'll learn a bit about how to model data in Aerospike, how to monitor it for issues, and how to optimize the underlying hardware. You'll get some basic information about Aerospike architecture, more depth on what makes it unique, and guidance on different methods to work with it to achieve optimal performance. In the end, you should have a solid foundation that will let you move to the next level and put Aerospike to work for you. First, let's take a look at getting it installed and building your first application.

## CHAPTER 2

Developing Your First Aerospike Application

Now that you know what Aerospike is, let's start writing our first program using Aerospike as the database. Aerospike supports multiple programming languages such as Java, C, C#, Python, and Node.js, but this book will focus on Java and Python. If you are following along, be aware that the Python client works on Mac and Linux, but not Windows. Otherwise, the concepts discussed will apply to all the programming languages Aerospike supports. For a full list of these languages, which client versions work with which Aerospike server, and what features are supported, take a look at the Aerospike Client Matrix (*https://oreil.ly/In66g*).

Installing Aerospike

There are two components of Aerospike that you will need to install. The first is the actual Aerospike database and the second includes the tools used to interact with it. The database install only includes these tools for Linux. If you are using Mac OS, and you would like the convenience of not having to call Docker first before each command in the tools package, a native version of the tools will be required.

Since Aerospike is designed for the Linux operating system, it will not run natively on either Windows or Mac OS. However, there are simple ways to run Aerospike on these machines.

Installing Aerospike on Windows or a Mac

Running the database on Windows or a Mac requires using a virtualization layer like Docker or VirtualBox to run Linux. Docker or a similar containerized solution is arguably easier to get started, so we will focus on that. (If you're using a full virtualization layer like VirtualBox, then follow the instructions for Linux installation.)

You can use Docker Desktop (*https://oreil.ly/l--AO*), which, at the time of writing, is free for personal use. However, many developers and organizations have concerns about the license of Docker Desktop and are turning to the free, open source Podman (*https://oreil.ly/NVbey*) instead. Podman can be configured as a drop-in replacement for Docker and has a nice user interface with Podman Desktop (*https://oreil.ly/FXQYm*), so this chapter will focus on Podman.

To install Podman Desktop follow the instructions at the Podman website for either Mac (*https://oreil.ly/kTbZK*) or Windows (*https://oreil.ly/3cymv*). Once you launch the software you will likely be prompted to install the Podman engine, which is a necessary step.

While you're in the user interface, you will want to enable Docker compatibility mode. This feature allows you to use Docker commands and have them processed by Podman. To do this, go to Settings in Podman Desktop (the cog icon in the lower left of the window), then select Preferences, and scroll down to "Docker Compatibility" under "Extension: Podman" on the right, or type "Docker" in the Preferences search bar. Enable this setting and then restart Podman Desktop. You should notice that "Docker Compatibility" now appears in the lower-left corner of the screen. See Figure 2-1 for an example.

You will need to install the Docker CLI to use Docker commands with Podman. On a Mac, this can be done with Homebrew using the following command:

```
brew install docker
```

On Windows you will need to install Docker Desktop (*https://oreil.ly/3LaFP*) to get access to the Docker CLI. At the time of writing using the Docker CLI with Podman running the containers is permissible with the Docker Desktop license, without a commercial license.

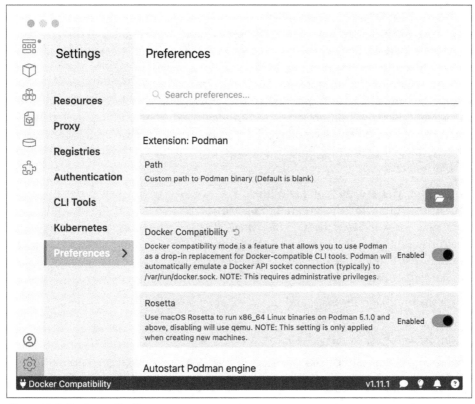

Figure 2-1. Podman Preferences

If you already have Docker installed and have used it, you might encounter conflicts between Docker and Podman. For example, you may see an error like this:

```
$ docker ps
Cannot connect to the Docker daemon at
unix:///Users/albert/.docker/run/docker.sock.
Is the docker daemon running?
```

This might be resolved by removing the *~/.docker* folder:

```
$ podman machine stop
$ rm -rf .docker/
$ podman machine start
Starting machine "podman-machine-default"
API forwarding listening on: /var/run/docker.sock
```

Installing the Aerospike database container

Once you've installed Podman and the Docker CLI, use it to pull down the latest copy of the Aerospike database and install it. There are two different versions of Aerospike: the fully open source Community Edition or the Enterprise Edition. The Aerospike Enterprise Edition includes all the features of the Community Edition plus other enterprise features like encryption at rest, compression, durable deletes, and so on. Aerospike Enterprise Edition is free to download and use for a one-node database, but clustering more than one node requires a commercial license. Multinode clusters are free in the Community Edition but lack some of the features of the Aerospike Enterprise Edition.

So that you can see the complete functionality, we're going to use the Aerospike Enterprise Edition for the programming part of this book, but either edition will work and we will draw distinctions when discussing features that are Aerospike Enterprise Edition only. If you do want to investigate the Community Edition, you can find instructions and downloads on the Aerospike Server Community Edition website (*https://oreil.ly/1E5Zd*).

To get the latest Docker image and start the Aerospike server, run:

```
docker run -tid --name aerospike -p 3000-3002:3000-3002
aerospike/aerospike-server-enterprise
```

This will pull down the latest version of the Aerospike database and start up a container. Let's look at the parameters to the Docker command:

- `run` tells Docker to launch a program.
- `-tid` specifies the program should run detached and interactively, so you can attach to the process later and look at logs later if you should choose to do so.
- `--name` gives the Docker process a name, so you can use this name to manage the process through Docker rather than using the container ID.
- `-p 3000-3002:3000-3002` exposes the container's ports of 3000, 3001, and 3002 to the corresponding ports on the underlying host machine. This means you can attach your favorite IDE to the database without needing to worry about the database running in a container. Port 3000 is the port that the client will talk to the server on, so it is most important from the developer perspective. Port 3001 is used for the "fabric"—the exchange of data between nodes in the cluster. Port 3002 is used for heartbeats, to allow the cluster to know if a node or set of nodes is no longer responsive.
- `aerospike/aerospike-server-enterprise` is the name of the image to download, in this case the Aerospike Enterprise Edition. At the time of writing, the latest version of Aerospike Enterprise Edition is 6.4.0.1.

To ensure this ran successfully, execute:

```
% docker ps
```

This should display something similar to the following:

```
CONTAINER ID IMAGE COMMAND CREATED STATUS PORTS NAMES
979765d925df aerospike/aerospike-server-enterprise "/usr/bin/as-tini-st…"
2 minutes ago Up 2 minutes 0.0.0.0:3000-3002->3000-3002/tcp,
:::3000-3002->3000-3002/tcp aerospike
```

If you look in your Podman Desktop, you should also be able to see the container `aerospike` running.

Installing tools

On a Mac, running the tools locally eliminates the need to run every command through `docker exec`, making the commands simpler. The download page at the Aerospike website (*https://oreil.ly/o1cGK*) allows you to download the tools natively with an intuitive user interface.

In the System dropdown, select "macOS" and make sure the selected option in the CPU dropdown is appropriate for your Mac—either Intel/AMD64 for Intel-based Macs, or ARM64 for Macs based on the "M" series of processors.

Once this download is complete, run the binary to be guided through the installation process. You can validate that the installation was successful by launching a terminal window and executing:

```
% asinfo -v build
6.4.0.1
```

Note that your output may be different based on which version you installed, but so long as you get a version returned, the install was successful.

The Aerospike tools do not run natively on Windows, so the best option for Windows users is to run them through the containers. The Aerospike container you started already has the tools installed. You can use the tools inside the container like so:

```
% docker exec -it aerospike 'asinfo -v build'
6.4.0.1
```

Installing Aerospike on Linux

Since Aerospike runs natively on Linux it is easy to install on this platform. Use a browser to navigate to the Aerospike downloads page (*https://oreil.ly/91eNP*). Here you will find a list of Aerospike versions available for download as shown in Figure 2-2. Select the right version, then download the file corresponding to your system. You can choose to either download the file or to copy a link to the file in case you prefer to use a tool like `wget` to download the file.

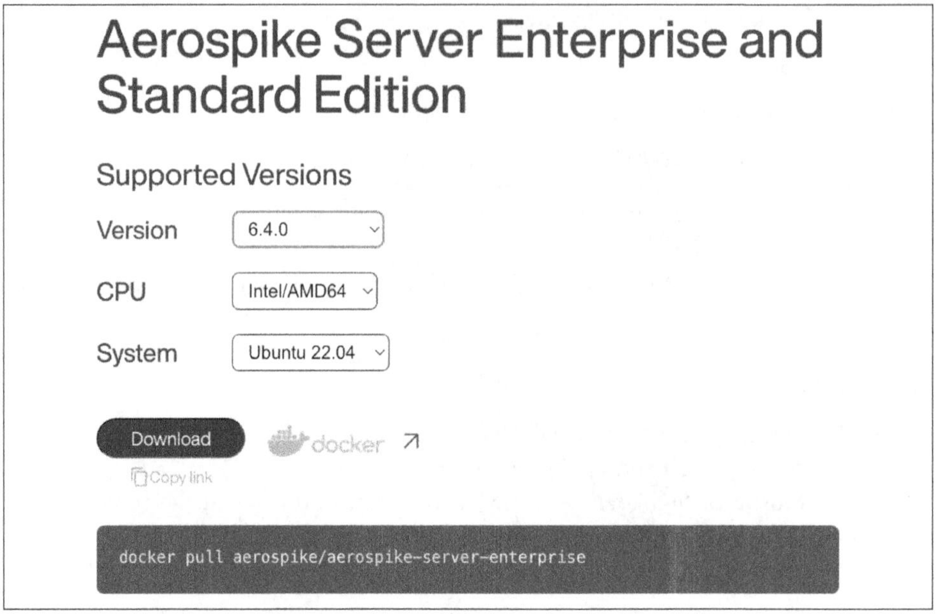

Figure 2-2. Aerospike download page

Once you've downloaded the server, untar it. Change to the appropriate subdirectory that was created as part of the tarball extraction. Finally, run:

```
% sudo ./asinstall
```

This will install Aerospike in the appropriate folders on your system, as well as the Aerospike tools.

On Linux, Aerospike is installed as a service to make maintaining the system easier. Depending on your Linux variant, either use the `service` or the `systemctl` command to check the status of the service and start it if needed:

```
% sudo systemctl status aerospike
% sudo systemctl start aerospike
```

Deployments Made Simple with AeroLab

If you're running in a virtualized environment like Docker/Podman or cloud environments like AWS or Google Cloud, the open source tool AeroLab (*https://oreil.ly/2zW-J*) can simplify deployments of different Aerospike environments.

Installing and configuring AeroLab

Navigate to AeroLab GitHub (*https://oreil.ly/6AtBT*), select the desired release, find your operating system under Assets, then download and install the image.

Once AeroLab is installed on your system, first tell it which backend to use. If you're using Podman, for example, you would use the following command:

```
aerolab config backend -t docker
```

AeroLab features context-sensitive help, so if you get stuck at any point, just put the word "help" after what you want to know. So, for example, if you knew you wanted to configure the backend but didn't know the options, you could enter:

```
aerolab config backend help
```

AeroLab would respond with appropriate help:

```
% aerolab config backend help
Usage:
  aerolab [OPTIONS] config backend [backend-OPTIONS] [help]
Global Options:
--beep                   cause the terminal to beep on exit; if specified multiple
                         times, will be once on success and >1 on failure
--beepf                  like beep, but does not trigger beep on success,
                         only failures
[backend command options]
-t, --type=              Supported backends: aws|docker|gcp
-p, --key-path=          AWS and GCP backends: specify a path to store SSH keys in,
                         default: ${HOME}/aerolab-keys/(default: ${HOME}/
                         aerolab-keys/)
-r, --region=            AWS backend: override default aws configured region
-P, --aws-profile=       AWS backend: provide a profile to use; setting this
                         ignores the AWS_PROFILE env variable
    --aws-nopublic-ip    AWS backend: if set, aerolab will not request public IPs,
                         and will operate on private IPs only
 -o, --project=          GCP backend: override default gcp configured project
 -a, --docker-arch=      set to either amd64 or arm64 to force a particular
                         architecture on docker; see https://github.com
                         /aerospike/aerolab/tree/master/docs/docker_multiarch.md
-d, --temp-dir=          use a non-default temporary directory
Available commands:
  help Print help
```

Using AeroLab

Once you have configured AeroLab you can use it to create a cluster. The simplest way is:

```
aerolab cluster create
```

This command will find the latest version of Aerospike Enterprise Edition from the public releases, download the image, create a container based on this image, and start up Aerospike. If you look in your Podman Desktop window or use `docker ps` at a command prompt, you should find one process with the name `aerolab-mydc_1`. AeroLab clusters have names, normally specified with `-n <cluster_name>` when referencing the cluster. Since that parameter was omitted on the preceding command, AeroLab defaulted the cluster name to `mydc`.

 AeroLab will create clusters in Docker/Podman and expose their ports to the host so you can connect to them through your IDE. Aerospike by default listens on port 3000, but AeroLab creates containers starting from port 3100. If you are connecting to a cluster started with AeroLab, be sure to change the port when connecting to the cluster, as you will see later in this chapter.

So instead of

```
IAerospikeClient client = new AerospikeClient(null
127.0.0.1", 3000);
```

you would use

```
IAerospikeClient client = new AerospikeClient(null,
"127.0.0.1", 3100);
```

To view the cluster you can run:

```
aerolab cluster list
```

This will show a set of information. Some of the most pertinent columns in the result would include:

```
CLUSTERS
ClusterName ... ExposedPort ...  AsdVer Arch Distro DistroVer ...
   mydc      ... 3100        ...  6.4.0.5 arm64 ubuntu 22.04   ...
```

You can see that the cluster name here is `mydc` (the AeroLab default), the node is listening on port 3100, and it's running Aerospike version 6.4.0.5 on Ubuntu 22.04.

You can easily deploy a single-node cluster with either Docker/Podman or AeroLab as these examples show. However, the command to do so is easier to remember using AeroLab and it is more flexible for various other deployment scenarios. For example, imagine that you wanted to create a five-node cluster of Aerospike Community Edition version 6.4.0 with the name source. This can be achieved using:

```
aerolab cluster create -n source -c 5 -v 6.4.0c
```

-n source tells AeroLab that the cluster should be known as source (rather than mydc), -c 5 specifies a node count of five nodes, and -v 6.4.0c says to use the Community Edition of Aerospike with version 6.4.0. Note that the c after the version number tells AeroLab that you want the Community Edition; if this is omitted then the Aerospike Enterprise Edition is assumed.

When this command has successfully completed, you will have a five-node Aerospike cluster up and running. Trying to do the same thing with Docker/Podman would require substantial amounts of configuration to ensure the containers know to form a distributed Aerospike cluster and can communicate with each other appropriately.

To connect to an AeroLab cluster running in Docker that has more than one node, you will need to pass a "services alternate" flag:

```
ClientPolicy cp = new ClientPolicy();
cp.useServicesAlternate=true;
IAerospikeClient client = new AerospikeClient(cp, "127.0.0.1", 3100);
```

The reason for this is due to the networking within the containers that form the cluster. They will communicate with each other on internal Docker addresses that are not visible to the host machine. Specifying useServicesAlternate tells the client to communicate with them on network ports it can see. More information can be found in the Aerospike documentation (*https://oreil.ly/McDku*).

AeroLab has a lot of features to help with Aerospike deployments. One of the most useful commands is the ability to connect to a node in the cluster, which can be done using:

```
aerolab attach shell [-n cluster_name]
```

Like most AeroLab commands, the command requires the name of the cluster, which will default to mydc. Given you created a one-node cluster with that name earlier in the chapter, you should just be able to run the following command to get a shell on that server:

```
aerolab attach shell
root@mydc-1:/#
```

Note that if you have multiple nodes in your cluster such as the source cluster created earlier, you can select the node to run the shell on by passing the --node (or -l) option. As usual, you can see all of the options for the command by putting help at the end of the command, in this case aerolab attach shell help. To attach to the third node in the source cluster, you could execute:

```
aerolab attach shell -n source --node 3
root@source-3:/#
```

Aerospike Terminology

Aerospike has a number of concepts that are similar to, but not exactly the same as, other databases you might be familiar with. To understand these concepts, let's compare Aerospike to a relational database management system (RDBMS).

In Figure 2-3 you can see the typical structure of a relational row-based database. The data is grouped into databases, with each database being logically isolated from one another. Each database contains tables where a table is a logical grouping of rows, aka records, such as Customer or Account.

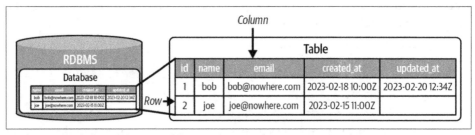

Figure 2-3. Relational data model

Tables have a schema in an RDBMS, and hence every row in the table has the same columns. This schema dictates what columns should exist, the types of the columns, whether null values are allowed, and so on.

Rows contain the data, which is broken down into columns, with each column holding a single piece of information. Since the schema enforces all rows having the same structure, if a piece of data is not needed, it still needs a null entry in the row. For example, Joe's row in Figure 2-3 does not have an "updated_at" entry, so this will be null.

In contrast, Aerospike's data model is shown in Figure 2-4.

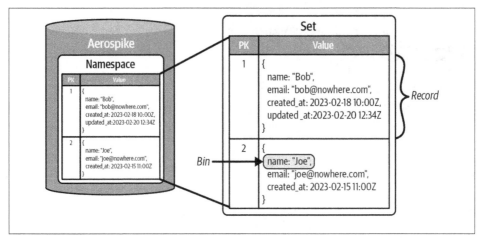

Figure 2-4. Aerospike's data model

The top-level storage concept is the *namespace*, a logical organization of named objects Aerospike is working with. In this case, the namespace functions similarly to a tablespace or a database in relational concepts. It defines the storage being used for the data and indexes, how many copies of the data to store across the cluster, and so on. Namespaces are typically isolated from each other so that if different namespaces store data on different SSDs, they do not suffer from "noisy neighbor" problems associated with the storage devices.

A set is a logical grouping of records, similar to a table in an RDBMS. While a table has a schema that strictly defines the structure of all rows in that table, Aerospike sets are schemaless and therefore can store either structured or unstructured data.

A record is akin to a row in a relational database. It contains a number of discrete items of data in bins (similar to a column in a relational database). Since Aerospike is schemaless, each record is self-describing and so can be thought of as similar to a map data type, with the bin name being the key to the map and the value being the bin's contents.

The value inside a bin can be a scalar like a string, integer, or float, or complex like a list or map. These lists and maps (collectively called collection data types, or CDTs for short) can be nested inside one another, allowing for arbitrarily complex data structures within a single bin. Table 2-1 summarizes the terminology for Aerospike versus an RDMBS.

Table 2-1. Aerospike to RDBMS equivalent terminology

Aerospike	RDBMS
Namespace	Database/Tablespace
Set	Table
Record	Record/Row
Bin	Field/Column

Note that in Figure 2-4, Record 2 does not have an "updated_at" field, similar to the RDBMS example in Figure 2-3. However, unlike the RDBMS, the value in Aerospike is not null; it is just not present in the record. As each record is self-describing, different records can have different numbers or types of bins. Similarly, different records can have different types in bins with the same name. For example, one record might have a bin called "data" containing an integer and another may have a bin with the same name containing a string. This is rare as the application that generates the data normally stores the same sort of data in records in the same set, hence effectively enforcing a schema on the set.

Also note that each bin inside a record has a known type. The type is set when the data is entered in that bin, and changing the contents of the bin will change the type. Consider the following Java snippet:

```
client.put(null, key, new Bin("data", 10));    // long
client.put(null, key, new Bin("data", 10.0));  // double
client.put(null, key, new Bin("data", "10"));  // String
```

In this case, the same bin is being set to three different values, although the representations are similar. In the first example, you're passing 10 (an integer) to the bin, so it will be stored as an integer. In the second example, the passed value is a double value, so Aerospike will store the value as a double, and in the last example the value will be stored as a string. Note that there is not an obvious API call to determine the type of a bin. The bin can be read and the contents examined, or the bin type can be determined using Expressions, which will be covered in Chapter 4.

Aerospike internally always stores integral values in a 64-bit integer, and floating-point values in a 64-bit double value. Hence there is no difference between storing 10 as an integer, a long, or a short, for example—Aerospike will treat them all identically.

The type of bin can affect the operations that can be performed on that bin. For example, if a string is stored in a bin, a string append operation could be performed on it but adding an integer to it could not. If the bin value is replaced with a new value of a different type, the type of the new bin determines the allowed operations going forward. While there are ways to cast bins to different types using Expressions, these are typically not needed as the application enforces a schema with the correct type on the bins.

Simple First Application

Now that you understand the data model, let's go and create a simple first Java program. In this case you're just going to connect to the database, insert a record into the Item set in the **test** namespace, then read that record back and print out information contained in the record:

```java
public class FirstProgram {
    public static void main(String[] args) {
        IAerospikeClient client = new AerospikeClient(null, "127.0.0.1", 3000);
        Key key = new Key("test", "item", 1);
        client.put(null, key, new Bin("name", "Stylish Couch"),
                new Bin("cost", 50000), new Bin("discount", 0.21));
        Record item = client.get(null, key);
        System.out.printf("%s costs $%.02f with a %d%% discount\n",
                item.getString("name"), item.getInt("cost")/100.0,
                (int)(100*item.getFloat("discount")));
        client.close();
    }
}
```

In Python:

```python
import aerospike

client = aerospike.client({'hosts':[('127.0.0.1', 3000)]}).connect()
key = ('test', 'item', 1)
bins = {
    'name': 'Stylish Couch',
    'cost': 50000,
    'discount': 0.21
}
client.put(key, bins)
(key_, meta, bins) = client.get(key)
print('Record:', bins)
client.close()
```

This program shows the Aerospike client driver in both Java and Python. For Java the driver will need to be imported. How to import the library depends on the build tool you use. For example, using Apache Maven, you would add a dependency similar to:

```
<dependency>
    <groupId>com.aerospike</groupId>
    <artifactId>aerospike-client</artifactId>
    <version>6.1.10</version>
</dependency>
```

In Gradle, this would be:

```
implementation group: 'com.aerospike', name: 'aerospike-client', version: '6.1.10'
```

For specifics on other languages or other build tools or to simply download the client as a JAR file, visit the Aerospike client download page (*https://oreil.ly/KN1OP*) and navigate to the appropriate language section. Note that the server version and the client version do not need to match, and it's typically best to use the latest version of both. The clients and servers try to maintain backward compatibility so you can update the server and keep the client version the same, or vice versa.

Now, let's examine our first program.

Establishing a Connection to the Database

The first thing you need to do is establish a connection to the database:

```
ClientPolicy clientPolicy = new ClientPolicy();
clientPolicy.user = "admin";
clientPolicy.password = "adminPassword";
IAerospikeClient client = new AerospikeClient(null, "127.0.0.1", 3000);
```

In Python:

```
client = aerospike.client({'hosts':[('127.0.0.1', 3000)]}).connect('admin',
'adminPassword')
```

Establishing a connection to the database requires just three parameters:

- The ClientPolicy dictates how to connect to the database. Almost all operations in Aerospike take a policy of one sort or another as the first argument and we will cover policies in detail shortly. This example passes a username and password to the cluster to allow logging in to a security-enabled cluster (an enterprise feature). Like all Aerospike policies, null can be passed here to tell Aerospike to use its defaults.

- An Aerospike server's host address. This can be a hostname, DNS address, or IP address.

- The port on the host that Aerospike is listening on. This is port 3000 by default.

Note that in a production system this code wouldn't be great. Aerospike is a clustered database, so there are typically multiple exactly identical machines that hold the data. This eliminates any single points of failure in the cluster. However, our code is connecting to just a single node, and if that node goes down the application cannot connect. A more robust constructor would pass multiple addresses and look more like the following:

```
IAerospikeClient client = new AerospikeClient(clientPolicy,
        new Host("172.17.0.2", 3000),
        new Host("172.17.0.3", 3000),
        new Host("172.17.0.4", 3000));
```

In Python:

```
config = {
    'hosts': [
        ('172.17.0.2', 3000),
        ('172.17.0.3', 3000),
        ('172.17.0.4', 3000)
    ]
}
```

These nodes are known as *seed hosts*. When the `AerospikeClient` is created, Aerospike starts at the first seed host in the list and attempts to establish a connection to it. If it cannot connect, it moves on to the next seed host, and so on. An exception is thrown if no connection can be established and all the seed hosts have been tried.

However, if one of the seed hosts resolves to a cluster, Aerospike uses this cluster as its database and no further seed hosts are attempted. The response back from the seed host contains information about all the nodes in the cluster. When the client receives this information, it then attempts to establish a pool of connections with each one of these nodes.

The Aerospike clusters are dynamic. Nodes can be added and removed at any time. Node removal can either be planned, such as taking a node down to patch its operating system, or unplanned, such as a hardware failure taking the node down. Hence the client needs to continually refresh its view of what nodes are in the cluster. This process is known as *tending the cluster*, which happens once per second by default. If the client has an inaccurate view of the cluster and sends a request to the wrong node, the cluster is smart enough to proxy that request to the node that can serve that piece of data.

At the end of the application the client should be closed with a call to the `close()` method to free up resources on both the client and server:

```
client.close();
```

Note that once a client has been closed, it cannot be used again. So if, for example, you have an online program that creates an `AerospikeClient` designed to run continuously and you then occasionally run a batch job that reuses the same client, the batch program should not call close() when it completes, as this will affect the online application.

Once created, the client is designed to be multithreaded. Typically, only a single client is needed in a single program; all requests to the database should use that same client. As you can see, creating a new AerospikeClient is an expensive operation—you potentially try multiple seed nodes, create connection pools, and initialize the thread that tends the cluster. So creating and closing clients will slow the application down dramatically.

Inserting and Retrieving Data

To insert or retrieve data from Aerospike by primary key (PK), a Key must be created. Keys have three components:

1. The namespace
2. The set name
3. The PK value

So, in this case, you could create a Key as follows:

```
Key key = new Key("test", "item", 1);
```

In Python:

```
key = ('test', 'item', 1)
```

The namespace is test and you're going to be using the record with primary key 1 in the item set.

To insert a record of data in the item set, Aerospike requires the policy, the key, and the data to insert:

```
client.put(null, key, new Bin("name", "Stylish Couch"),
            new Bin("cost", 50000), new Bin("discount", 0.21));
```

In Python:

```
bins = {
    'name': 'Stylish Couch',
    'cost': 50000,
    'discount': 0.21
}
client.put(key, bins)
```

This will create a new record in the database with three columns—name (a string), cost (an integer), and discount (a float).

In Aerospike, all record modifying operations by default are UPSERTs—if the record exists, it will be updated; if the record does not exist, it will be created. Chapter 3 will cover this in more detail. Similarly, if the set does not exist, Aerospike will automatically create it when data is inserted.

Aerospike is also case sensitive, so, for example, the set `testSet` is different from the set `TestSet`. However, keywords like `SELECT` are case insensitive when using tools like Aerospike Quick Look, introduced later in the chapter.

To retrieve a record, supply the policy and the key you want to retrieve:

```
Record item = client.get(null, key);
```

In Python:

```
(key_, meta, bins) = client.get(key);
```

Note that the `Record` class being used here is `com.aerospike.client.Record`. Java 16 introduced `java.lang.Record`, which some IDEs will try to use by default, so you will need to explicitly list `com.aerospike.client.Record` in the import statements for the class.

The returned `Record` will contain all the values in the record that can be retrieved by invoking **get** methods. If the type of data being retrieved is known, you can use specific methods like `getString()`, `getInt()`, and so on. If the type of the value being returned is unknown, you can use the `getValue()` method.

Using Aerospike Quick Look

Congratulations! You've now written your first program to use Aerospike. You inserted a record and retrieved it, validating that the record was correctly inserted. It is possible to view and change the records in an Aerospike database without writing code as well. One of the methods of doing that is to use Aerospike Quick Look (AQL). This uses a SQL-like dialect to manipulate the data. Note however that this is not a SQL tool, and while some commands look like SQL, general SQL queries are not supported.

From a terminal, AQL can be started in interactive mode simply by executing `% aql`.

aql will try to connect on localhost (127.0.0.1) by default. You can connect to a different IP address by using the -h option. For example, your Docker container running Aerospike might be at 172.17.0.2 and you can connect to that using % aql -h 172.17.0.2.

If you're running a cluster out of AeroLab, you can change the port by placing the desired port after the hostname separated by a colon. For example: % aql -h localhost:3100.

This should give some basic information:

```
% aql
Seed: 127.0.0.1
User: None
Config File: /etc/aerospike/astools.conf /
Users/book/.aerospike/astools.conf
Aerospike Query Client
Version 8.1.0
C Client Version 6.3.0
Copyright 2012-2024 Aerospike. All rights reserved.
aql>
```

From there you can query the data using AQL:

```
aql> select * from test.item where pk =1
```

This should give the data for this specific PK:

```
+----+-----------------+-------+----------+
| PK | name            | cost  | discount |
+----+-----------------+-------+----------+
| 1  | "Stylish Couch" | 50000 | 0.21     |
+----+-----------------+-------+----------+
1 row in set (0.000 secs)
OK
```

You can also insert a new record or update the existing record, using the same semantics for both, as there is no difference between an INSERT and an UPDATE in Aerospike. To update a record, use:

```
aql> insert into test.item(Pk, cost) values (1, 60000)
OK, 1 record affected.

aql> select * from test.item where pk =1
+----+-----------------+-------+----------+
| PK | name            | cost  | discount |
+----+-----------------+-------+----------+
| 1  | "Stylish Couch" | 60000 | 0.21     |
+----+-----------------+-------+----------+
1 row in set (0.001 secs)
OK
```

The command merged the updated bin (cost) with the existing record, preserving the existing columns, which were not updated.

Inserting a new record requires providing all the bins:

```
aql> insert into test.item(PK, name, cost, discount)
values (2, "Blue Chair", 7399, 0.03)
```

All records can then be viewed:

```
aql> select * from test.item
+----+----------------+-------+----------+
| PK | name           | cost  | discount |
+----+----------------+-------+----------+
|  2 | "Blue Chair"   | 7399  | 0.03     |
|  1 | "Stylish Couch"| 60000 | 0.21     |
+----+----------------+-------+----------+
2 rows in set (0.164 secs)
```

AQL is useful for basic data manipulation, but it is a long way from a full SQL implementation. We list some of the most common statements in AQL in Table 2-2.

Table 2-2. Common AQL commands

Command	Usage
help	Displays what commands AQL supports. Note that different versions of AQL may support different commands; using help will always show the supported commands.
INSERT INTO <ns>[.<set>] (PK, <bins>) VALUES (<key>, <values>)	Insert or update the specified bins in the specified record. Since all INSERTs are really UPSERTs, there is no specific UPDATE command. Note the use of PK to refer to the primary key. For example: insert into test.testSet(PK, name, age) values (1, 'Tim', 312)
DELETE FROM <ns>[.<set>] WHERE PK = <key>	Delete a single record. For example: delete from test.testSet where PK = 1
SELECT <bins> FROM <ns>[.<set>]	Retrieves all the records in a set and displays them. For big sets, this normally times out as the timeout default is one second. For example: select * from test.testSet
SELECT <bins> FROM <ns>[.<set>] WHERE PK = <key>	Retrieves a single record from the Aerospike database. For example: select name, age from test.testSet where PK = 1
SELECT <bins> FROM <ns>[.<set>] WHERE <bin> = <value>	Selects records that match a given criteria. Note that a secondary index must be defined on the bin in the where clause (secondary indexes will be discussed in Chapter 4). For example: select * from test.testSet where name = 'Tim'
SHOW NAMESPACES	Shows details of all the namespaces in the database.

Command	Usage
SHOW SETS	Shows details of all the sets in the database.
SET OUTPUT JSON|RAW|TABLE	Set the format of the output. Defaults to "table".

As previously noted, Aerospike is case sensitive: table1 is different from Table1, which is different from TABLE1. However, AQL keywords like SELECT, DELETE, FROM, and so on are NOT case sensitive. Also, AQL is designed to give a familiar, SQL-like dialect for a few commands as shown earlier, but it is not designed for bulk data insertion nor anything substantially more complicated than what is shown in Table 2-2 or in the output of the aql help command.

Policies

Almost all of the calls you have reviewed so far have required a policy. Policies dictate how a particular call should behave, such as what happens if there is an issue with the network, or what to do if the record already exists. We have very conveniently passed null to these so far, so the defaults were used, but let's see why policies are important. For this discussion we're going to focus on the put command:

```
client.put(null, key, new Bin("name", "Stylish Couch"),
            new Bin("cost", 50000), new Bin("discount", 0.21));
```

The first parameter here, which is null in the preceding statement, is a WritePolicy, which subclasses the Policy class. The Policy class controls some general parameters that are useful on the majority of calls, such as networking information. Some of the most important fields in this class are shown in Table 2-3.

Table 2-3. Some of the more commonly used fields in the Policy class

Field	Default	Description
socketTimeout	30000	When sending a transaction to the server, how long to wait in milliseconds before declaring a timeout has occurred. This may trigger retries based on the following settings.
maxRetries	2	If a timeout occurs when sending to the server, how many retries to attempt before giving up. This defaults to 2 for reads, 0 for writes, and 5 for scan/queries.
sleepBetweenRetries	0	If a transaction can be retried, how long to wait in milliseconds between the retries.
totalTimeout	1000	The total time in milliseconds to wait for the transaction and all retries before giving up. Note that if this parameter is exceeded a Timeout exception will be thrown to the application, even if the number of retries has not been exceeded.
compress	false	Whether to compress data between the client and the server. For large operations this may reduce network traffic at the cost of CPU.
filterExp	null	Whether to filter out operations on the server based on a filter expression. Expressions will be discussed in more detail later in the book.

These network settings, in particular, are very important for production applications. They dictate how the client layer should respond if the server is not responding in time. For example, if a server dies due to a hardware failure, there is a brief period where the client and the rest of the cluster do not know that the server is down and will still route traffic to it. This can cause timeouts on the client, but these settings can allow the client to retry the operation if desired.

The WritePolicy subclass itself has some other useful properties for the application. The main ones are listed in Table 2-4.

Table 2-4. Some of the more commonly used fields in the WritePolicy class

Field	Default	Description
durableDelete	false	When a record is explicitly deleted, should a tombstone marker be placed in the record or should it be quickly expunged? In some edge cases, expunged records can reappear in the database. Durable deletes are an enterprise-only feature at the moment, but they are recommended for data whose integrity is paramount.
expiration	0	Records in Aerospike can be automatically removed by the system. This field is the number of seconds that records should be kept for. After this time the records will automatically be removed by Aerospike. If this field is -1, the records will live forever unless explicitly deleted. If this field is 0, the default time to live specified in the namespace will be used.
generation generationPolicy	0	These two fields are used together to allow applications to implement thread-safe read-modify-write cycles on the database using optimistic concurrency. We'll discuss this in more detail in later chapters.
recordExistsAction	UPDATE	When an operation changes a record, how should that change be merged with the existing record if there is one.

To illustrate how these policies can be used, consider the write in our simple program:

```
client.put(null, key, new Bin("name", "Stylish Couch"),
                new Bin("cost", 50000), new Bin("discount", 0.21));
```

Since the policy is null the defaults will be used, and the default recordExistsAction is UPDATE. This will update the record if it exists and create a new record if it doesn't. Let's say that the business requirements were to only create a record with this call; if the record already exists an exception should be thrown. This corresponds to a recordExistsAction of CREATE_ONLY. To implement this, you would change the code as follows:

```
WritePolicy writePolicy = new WritePolicy(client.getWritePolicyDefault());
writePolicy.recordExistsAction = RecordExistsAction.CREATE_ONLY;
client.put(writePolicy, key, new Bin("name", "Stylish Couch"),
                new Bin("cost", 50000), new Bin("discount", 0.21));
```

In Python:

```
writePolicy = {'exists': aerospike.POLICY_EXISTS_CREATE}
client.put(key, bins, policy=writePolicy)
```

In this case you need to create a new WritePolicy. Suppose you were to just instantiate a new WritePolicy by using:

```
WritePolicy writePolicy = new WritePolicy();
```

This would work, but the parameters' values would be those hardcoded as defaults in the Aerospike client driver. It is quite normal for applications to use a set of timeout fields that make sense for the SLAs in their environment. These settings should be the starting point for all calls, and calls can override these settings as the specific calls dictate.

In order to do this, the ClientPolicy has a set of default parameters, one for each of the different policy types. Creating a new WritePolicy based off the writePolicy Default will create a separate policy instance you can use for this specific call without affecting concurrent write calls in other threads while at the same time preserving most of the default settings, with only one change.

The code then sets the recordExistsAction to CREATE_ONLY. The Aerospike server will check to see if a record with that key already exists and it will throw an exception if it does. If no such record exists, the new record will be inserted into the database. Note that this is done atomically—there is no possibility of another thread creating the record between when the server checks for the existence of the record and when it inserts the record into the database.

Summary

In this chapter you installed Aerospike and wrote your first program. You learned how to read and write records and use the AQL tool to inspect and change the data. Finally, you learned about policies and how these can affect operations. In the next chapter, you'll dive more into the features of Aerospike from the client's perspective.

## CHAPTER 3

Basic Operations

In Chapter 2, we illustrated what an introductory sample application might look like. We briefly discussed establishing connections, retrieving data, and inserting data. In this chapter, we will dive into all the basic operations you'll use when putting Aerospike to work, such as creating, reading, updating, and deleting. These operations are the heart of day-to-day usage. You'll use what you learn in this chapter every day you use Aerospike.

We will also discuss time-to-live (TTL), which helps with data lifecycle management, work more with `WritePolicy` and `Policy`, and explore various data types and how to use them. In particular, you'll see how the Aerospike client interface handles the data types for you in many cases, making data movement between systems easier.

CRUD Operations

Create, read, update, and delete (CRUD) are the four fundamental operations of interacting with any database, including Aerospike, and you will need them to get started with the basics. Before discussing the basic operations in depth, we should talk about the data types that can be used in Aerospike natively and the data lifecycle options available.

Data Types

A record in Aerospike can contain one or more bins. When created, Aerospike bins are of certain data types. It is important to know the various data types so you can make informed decisions based on their capabilities and limitations as well as the data size costs.

The Aerospike client driver's built-in conversion allows you to create these data types independent of the language that created the data or input it. In other words, the data types in Aerospike are language agnostic, which makes it easier to apply new use cases to the data later. Table 3-1 describes Aerospike data types.

Table 3-1. Data types

Data type	Description
Integer	64-bit numerical values. Can be signed or unsigned. Used for whole numbers positive and negative (e.g., 42, -12).
Boolean	Holds a value of true or false.
Double	Used for storing fractional values or numbers with a decimal point. GPS coordinates, pricing, weather data such as temperatures, and weight are good examples (e.g., 37.4212, -122.0988).
String	Stores characters encoded as UTF-8, in an opaque byte array. Any combination of spaces, letters, and numbers could be represented as a string (e.g., "Aerospike is fast," "Tim," or "Pineapple42 themed backpack").

Map	A HashMap or dictionary-like data structure. Stores a relationship between a key and a value. Keys within a map are unique, with duplicates not allowed, so all values associated with that key are in one place. Keys in the map must be a scalar data type (string, integer, or blob only) and values can be scalar or collection types. Nesting is allowed. For example:
	
	`myMapBin: {`
	  `"Aerospike": "Fast"`
	  `"Product1234": "OReilly canned beans",`
	  `23: True,`
	  `255: [1,2,2,3]`
	  `}`

List	An array-type data structure, similar to a map in that it is a collection that can be operated on. It is distinct from the map type in that a list does not have a key to value relationship, and there can be duplicates of the data. Entries inside a list can either be scalar data types or collection data types as nesting is allowed. Some examples: a list of strings, a list of dictionaries, or even a list of lists or list of maps. For example:
	
	`pageViews: [`
	  `1691950585,`
	  `1691953456,`
	  `1691958589`
	  `]`
	
	List indexes are 0-based. Lists may be sorted or unsorted, configurable at write time. Also, list elements do not need to be homogenous, so a list like `[1691950585, "Tim", 0.42, true]` is perfectly valid.

Blob	Binary data, raw bytes. This data type might be chosen to store raw bytes due to a language-specific structure, for example, if you stored a compressed serialized dictionary, bloom filter, or in-house data type.
GeoJSON	Geometry objects, for geospatial matches (e.g., find if a point is within 42 miles of another point).
HyperLogLog	Probabilistic data type, used to count the members of a set or unions of a set (e.g. count of users who have an interest in "Computers" and "Furniture").

Data Lifecycle

If your data has a limited useful lifetime and will eventually need to be deleted and cleaned up, you should set a *time-to-live (TTL)* on the record by setting an *expiration* value in the WritePolicy while performing a write operation.

The TTL is the number of seconds until the server expires the record, deleting it automatically, and is updated when a write occurs on that record, which refreshes its lifetime. A server configuration parameter called nsup-period controls how often Aerospike cleans up records that should be expired. The default value is 0, which disallows setting TTL on records. Attempting to write a record with an expiration when the server does not allow TTL will result in an exception:

```
WritePolicy writePolicy = new WritePolicy();
writePolicy.expiration = 100;
client.put(writePolicy, key, new Bin("mybinname", "mybinvalue"));

Exception com.aerospike.client.AerospikeException: Error
22,1,0,30000,1000,0,BB9A328EA05C062 127.0.0.1 3101: Operation not allowed
at this time
```

If you wish to set a positive WritePolicy expiration value, you'll need to change the nsup-period in the Aerospike server to a nonzero value. A good starting value for nsup-period is 120 seconds if you are unsure of where to start but know you need a TTL.

Setting a TTL on your records is optional and can be specified for each write operation. There are also special flags you can use to prevent the TTL from being extended during a write. You can reference Table 3-2 for a summary of the Aerospike client driver WritePolicy expiration values and their effects.

Table 3-2. WritePolicy expiration value, client driver

WritePolicy expiration value	Effect
−2	Do not change the TTL while writing.
−1	Never expire.
0	Use the server configuration default-ttl for the namespace.
Values greater than 0	TTL in seconds: how long the record should exist in Aerospike.

Some datasets and applications may prefer this to be controlled by external logic, via some batch process or coordinated cleanup process, for example. If you need full control over how data gets deleted, or do not wish for it to be automatically cleaned up, you may set a WritePolicy expiration value of −1. The reason for choosing to disable expiration, with a default server configuration nsup-period=0, is to ensure that automatic cleanup and deletion of data is an opt-in experience. No data will be deleted unless you specifically define it to be.

 Setting the WritePolicy expiration value in the client to 0 means that data will expire in the amount of seconds defined by the default-ttl parameter on the server. However, setting default-ttl on the server to 0 means "never expire." These are similarly named but distinct configurations. These are separately documented in the Server Configuration reference for the default-ttl parameter, and in the Client API documentation for the WritePolicy.

Create

You *can* create a record in Aerospike with the put client method. You will need an AerospikeClient object to use the put method as described in Chapter 2. The AerospikeClient object is available in a number of different languages:

```
Key myKey = new Key("test", "item_set", 10012);
Bin myBin = new Bin("description", "Stylish Couch");

client.put(null, myKey, myBin);
```

In Python:

```
key = ('test', 'item_set', 10012)
bin = {'description': 'Stylish Couch'}
client.put(key, bin)
```

If you fetch this record, you'll see something like:

```
(gen:1),(exp:0),(bins:(description:Stylish Couch))
```

This example excludes the WritePolicy. The WritePolicy controls much of how a write works, such as defining the data expiration value, timeout, and what happens if the record already exists. As you can see from the fetched record, the expiration shows up as exp:0, meaning the record will never expire. If you want to pass a WritePolicy to set an expiration, and you've already configured the server with a nonzero nsup-period, you must pass that WritePolicy during your put command:

```
WritePolicy writePolicy = new WritePolicy();
writePolicy.expiration = 100;
Key myKey = new Key("test", "item_set", 10012);
Bin myBin = new Bin("description", "Stylish Couch");
client.put(writePolicy, myKey, myBin);
```

In Python:

```python
write_policy = {'expiration': 100}
key = ('test', 'item_set', 10012)
bin = {'description': 'Stylish Couch'}
client.put(key, bin, policy=write_policy)
```

Reference your client API documentation for the full list of `WritePolicy` options.

When writing a record, you may want to store it using a specific data type. Using the Aerospike client driver simplifies this process. Aerospike's driver assigns the data type to the bin that matches the source and inserts the data. If the bin is assigned a dictionary data type, such as HashMap in Java or dictionary in Python, the client will write that as an Aerospike `map` data type. Similarly, Java or Python `lists` will be assigned an Aerospike `list` data type.

Let's walk through an example of writing a map data type in Aerospike, and then printing it back out. First, you define our HashMap in Java, or a dictionary in Python, and put data in it.

Then you create an Aerospike bin, with no data type specified, and write the record to Aerospike. The Aerospike client driver's built-in conversion automatically matches the data type, which allows for storage of these collection types independent of the language that created the data or input it.

Next, you retrieve the data from the Aerospike bin and print it out. Printing displays the data, showing that it is unchanged by the round trip.

```java
// Define our product as a map
Map<String, Object> product = new HashMap<>();
product.put("name", "stylish couch");
product.put("productid", 123);
product.put("purchasable", true);

// Convert the map into an Aerospike Bin
Bin productBin = new Bin("product", product);

// Write the record to Aerospike
client.put(null, key, productBin);

// Read the record back from the database
Record record = client.get(null, key);

// fetch the Map bin out of the record, store as a Map
Map retrievedMap = record.getMap("product");

// Print the value of the bin
System.out.println(retrievedMap);

// Produces an output of:
// {productid=123, name=stylish couch, purchasable=true}
```

In Python:

```python
# Define an example dictionary
product = {
"name": "stylish couch",
"productid": 123,
"purchasable": True
}

# Define the bins to write
record = {
"product": product
}

# Write the record to Aerospike
client.put(key, record)

# Read the record back from the database
(key_, metadata, bins) = client.get(key)

# Print
print(bins)

# Produces an output of:
# {'product': {'name': 'stylish couch', 'productid': 123, 'purchasable': True}}
```

In Chapter 4, we will also discuss sending operations and expressions that help you interact with these data types without downloading them into the application for manipulation and inspection. This can greatly increase the efficiency, simplicity, and thread-safety of your application.

Read

Reading a record can be done using the get client method. The Policy is optional and can be defined to control things like timeouts, retries, and consistency level. You can also specify which bins you want to be retrieved, which will save resources if only a portion of the record is needed.

 As covered in Chapter 2, the Policy class is the superclass of other policy classes like WritePolicy and BatchPolicy, so they all inherit the timeout, retries, and other settings. While the put operation uses a WritePolicy, the get operation just uses a Policy not a ReadPolicy.

You can create a record with multiple bins:

```
Key myKey = new Key("test", "item_set", 10012);
Bin myBin = new Bin("description", "Stylish Couch");
Bin mySecondBin = new Bin("price", 23.04);
client.put(null, myKey, myBin, mySecondBin);
```

Then fetch just one of the bins that are stored in the database:

```
Record myRecord = client.get(null, myKey, "price");
System.out.printf("Got record: %s\n", myRecord)
```

This results in:

```
Got record: (gen:1),(exp:0),(bins:(price:23.04))
```

Reading the entire record transfers more data over:

```
Record myRecord = client.get(null, myKey);
System.out.printf("Got record: %s\n", myRecord);
```

You can see all the bins were transferred in this call, as a specific bin wasn't called out:

```
Got record: (gen:1),(exp:0),(bins:(description:Stylish Couch),(price:23.04))
```

The bin selection feature is not available in the current Aerospike Python driver, so you will need to use `client.select` or select out of the record dictionary after retrieving all the data locally:

```
(record_key, metadata, bins) = client.select(key, ['price'])
```

When reading a record from Aerospike, the application receives metadata from the server about the record. This metadata shows us the *generation* of the record and the *expiration*. The *generation* is a counter on the server, and the *expiration* shows the current TTL of the record that was read.

You can use the generation for conflict resolution and a *generation-sensitive* write pattern is usually used for check-and-set (CAS) writes—a method to avoid having multiple processes modify the same data in a distributed or multithreaded application using optimistic locking. The generation counter represents the number of times a record was modified, even if it was only to modify the TTL. This can be useful for ensuring a record has not been modified by another thread or application since it was last read.

There is an upper bound or limit to the generation counter, which, when reached, wraps around by resetting to 1.

The CAS pattern takes advantage of the metadata returned by a read, and the Gener ationPolicy setting of the WritePolicy. When you read the record with a simple get statement, you set an integer variable equal to the record's Generation property value. Then, you modify the data locally within our application. Then you set the WritePolicy to only write data if the current generation is equal to what it was the last time the data was read. You set the current generation to the value in the variable. Then write the data:

```
// Read the record to be updated
Record record = client.get(null, key);

// Get the current generation of the record
int currentGeneration = record.generation;

// Modify the data based on your requirements
// ...

// Perform the write operation with an expected generation
WritePolicy writePolicy = new WritePolicy();
writePolicy.generationPolicy = GenerationPolicy.EXPECT_GEN_EQUAL;
writePolicy.generation = currentGeneration; // Set the expected generation

// Update the record with the modified data
client.put(writePolicy, key, updatedBins);
```

In Python:

```
# Read the record to be updated
(_, metadata, record) = client.get(key)

# Get the current generation of the record
current_generation = metadata.generation

# Modify the data based on your requirements
# ...

# Perform the write operation with an expected generation
write_policy = {'gen': aerospike.POLICY_GEN_EQ}
write_policy['gen_value'] = current_generation # Set the expected generation

# Update the record with the modified data
client.put(key, updated_bins, policy=write_policy)
```

If the data was modified by another thread or application in between when the database read it and when the application went to write the modified data back, it will fail and throw an error that you can handle in your code:

```
Exception com.aerospike.client.AerospikeException: Error
3,1,0,30000,1000,0,BB9F6DDDD0EC32E 127.0.0.1 3100: Generation error
```

This keeps two different threads or applications from modifying the same data unintentionally.

Update

Updates are done using the same method as write operations, by using `put`. When you perform a `put` against an existing record, the default behavior is to perform an `UPSERT`. This means that Aerospike creates the record if it does not exist, but if it does exist, Aerospike will keep any existing data already on the record aside from the bin or bins you are operating on. If you have an existing record with some bins you aren't modifying and use the default update policy, those bins remain unchanged on the record.

This behavior is controlled via the `WritePolicy.recordExistsAction` specified when a `put` is called in Java. There is a similar selection in the Python client, but not under a specific enum, which can be referenced in Table 3-3 or in the API documentation (*https://oreil.ly/i5SfO*) under "Existence Policy Options" under the "aerospike" section. Though the specific implementations vary, this behavior modifier is present in all client drivers.

Table 3-3. `WritePolicy.RecordExistsAction`

Java	Python	Behavior
`RecordExistsAction.` `CREATE_ONLY`	`aerospike.POLICY_` `EXISTS_CREATE`	Create the record only if it does not exist. Throw an exception if it already exists.
`RecordExists` `Action.REPLACE`	`aerospike.POLICY_` `EXISTS_CREATE_` `OR_REPLACE`	Replace a record completely if it exists; otherwise create it.
`RecordExists` `Action.UPDATE`	`aerospike.POLICY_` `EXISTS_IGNORE`	Update a record if it exists; otherwise create it. This is the default behavior of all client drivers.
`RecordExists` `Action.REPLACE_ONLY`	`aerospike.POLICY_` `EXISTS_REPLACE`	Only replace a record completely if it exists. Throw an exception if the record does not exist.
`RecordExists` `Action.UPDATE_ONLY`	`aerospike.POLICY_` `EXISTS_UPDATE`	Only update a record if it exists. Throw an exception if it does not.

To illustrate how to use these policies and what their exceptions might look like, let's go through an example using `CREATE_ONLY`.

First, you set the policy to only create new records and throw an error if the record already exists. In Java, this is the `RecordExistsAction.CREATE_ONLY` setting. In Python, it's `aerospike.POLICY_EXISTS_CREATE`. Then, write the data. Assuming it doesn't already exist, it should simply write the data without error:

```
// Create the WritePolicy and set it to fail if the record already exists.
WritePolicy wp = new WritePolicy();
wp.recordExistsAction = RecordExistsAction.CREATE_ONLY;

// Write the data
client.put(wp, myKey, myBin);
```

In Python:

```
# Create the WritePolicy and set it to fail if the record already exists.
Create only.
wp = {
'exists': aerospike.POLICY_EXISTS_CREATE
}

# Write the data using the WritePolicy
client.put(my_key, my_bin, policy=wp)
```

If you ran this example program twice with the same key, the record would fail to be written the second time as it already exists. It would also throw an exception. The exception will look like this:

```
Exception in thread "main" com.aerospike.client.AerospikeException: Error
5,1,0,30000,1000,0,BB9020011AC4202 127.0.0.1 3000: Key already exists
```

 As you can see from Table 3-3, there is an option called replace. This will delete any existing data on a particular key that is not being rewritten by the client. If you had four bins on a record and then wrote three bins to the record using the replace policy, that fourth bin would be deleted since you are "replacing" the entire record. It may help to think of replace as "replace the entire record with this write."

Delete

The main method to delete an entire record is using the delete (Java) or remove (Python) client methods:

```
client.delete(null, myKey);
```

In Python:

```
client.remove(my_key);
```

There is an optional WritePolicy used for *durable deletes*, an Aerospike Enterprise Edition feature that offers a way to *tombstone* deletes. A tombstone marks that a record has been deleted that once existed with this key, so there is no way the records could be accidentally recovered in some event like a power outage.

Lightweight Operations

While it is possible to always write some data to a bin to refresh the record's TTL, you can do better. If you only need to refresh a record's TTL, you do not need to rewrite the entire record. Similarly, if you want to check if a record exists you do not need to fetch the entire record. These functionalities can be covered in a lighter way using the touch and exists methods the client driver provides.

The touch operation is a lightweight way of updating a record's metadata such as the TTL or generation. This is primarily used to refresh a record at read time to ensure it remains live. The touch operation only sends metadata and WritePolicy to the server, making it a very lightweight operation for the client.

In this example, you extend the TTL for a day (86,400 seconds):

```
WritePolicy writePolicy = new WritePolicy();
writePolicy.expiration = 86400;
client.touch(writePolicy, myKey);
```

In Python:

```
client.touch(my_key, 86400)
```

The exists function is similar in that it only transfers metadata across the network to the client. This is used to get a Boolean True or False signal on the client application to determine if the record exists:

```
client.exists(null, myKey);
```

In Python, this would be:

```
client.exists(my_key)
```

Note that exists returns whether the server contained that record at the time the call was executed. By the time the client receives the response from this call, it is possible that the value is incorrect due to there being multiple client instances. For example, one thread executes an exists call to see if a record exists, as it needs to create the record only if it does not already exist. At the time the server processed the API call the record did not exist, so False is returned. However, milliseconds later another client creates that record. The original client believes they can safely create the record when they cannot.

For this reason, exists is rarely used; normally a RecordExistsAction performs the same function but with atomic guarantees. In this example, the correct way to handle this situation would be to use a RecordExistsAction of CREATE_ONLY.

Batch

If there is a need to read or write many records at once, the batch-type operations may be most suitable. To perform a batch read operation, you need to create a list or array of keys you want to fetch and then you can pass that into the client.get method.

In this example, you do exactly that, first creating an array of the keys that you wish to read, then reading them all at once. Note that in Python, this is a different command: get_many, rather than the simple get:

```
Key[] keys = new Key[] {
new Key("test", "testset", "key1"),
new Key("test", "testset", "key2"),
new Key("test", "testset", "key3")
};

Records[] records = client.get(null, keys);
```

In Python:

```
keys = [
('test', 'testset', 'key1'),
('test', 'testset', 'key2'),
('test', 'testset', 'key3')
]

records = client.get_many(keys)
```

When you execute this, any of the records retrieved can be located positionally in the Records array. That means for key1 in this example, you would expect Records[0] to contain the data for it.

In Java, if the record is not found, then position 0 would be null, while in Python, you would see a None entry in the list. After you execute this and find records, you can interact with the records the same way you would while doing a single record read operation.

There are also ways to batch write operations and delete operations, which we'll cover in Chapter 4.

Summary

In this chapter, you learned how to perform CRUD operations to read, write, update, and delete. You explored how to work with the various data types, including how to create most of them, with the exception of the GeoJSON and HyperLogLog data types. These data types will require a more in-depth exploration than this introductory chapter addresses.

You learned about the behavior of write operations and how to control the behavior depending on if the record exists, as well as how to set and update the lifetime and the generation of a record. In the next chapter, you will look at the more advanced operations and techniques you can use to interact with Aerospike.

## CHAPTER 4

Advanced Operations

So far you have looked at Aerospike's basic operations, primarily reading and writing data. We have discussed how data is stored in bins and that multiple bins can be read or written in a single call. What you're going to look at now is some operations that go beyond those basics.

First, you'll look at a few of the many capabilities of the operate() command. In particular, you'll see how to add, append, and update data in some of the more complex data types such as lists and maps. Then, you'll learn some of the basics of how to use expressions to create conditional writes and derived reads, among other interesting data operations. You'll be introduced to more advanced batch operations, secondary indexes, multiple predicate queries, and a host of other aspects of using Aerospike.

The operate() Command

One of the most powerful commands on a single record is the operate() command. In fact, it is so powerful that all other single record commands are just syntactic sugar that wrap the operate() command. If you have been following along with the examples in this book so far, you have actually used this command, albeit wrapped in a get() or put() method.

operate() allows you to perform an arbitrary complex list of operations on a single record, taking a list of Operation classes containing the appropriate actions. So for example, in a single call, you could insert one bin, add 10 to the contents of another bin, work out the size of a map in a third bin, and so on. The basic syntax for the command is:

```
public Record operate(WritePolicy policy, Key key, Operation ... operations);
```

If you're not familiar with Java the "..." is the *varargs* operator, allowing an arbitrary number of parameters to be passed. So one argument could be passed or a hundred— it's up to you.

For illustrative purposes, let's say you're building a shopping cart application. The record for a user contains the items in the cart, a count of the items, and the total cost of the items. For this first example, you will assume that the items in the cart are simply stored in a string.

So, you could create a record similar to:

```
Key key = new Key("test", "cart", 1);
client.put(null, key,
      new Bin("items", "shoes,"),
      new Bin("totalItems", 1),
      new Bin("cost", 59.25));
```

As you saw earlier, this would create a key that references item 1 in the "cart" set (table) in the "test" namespace. A record would be written to the key that contains three bins with the values specified. This would yield a record similar to:

```
aql> select * from test.cart;
+----------+------------+-------+
| items    | totalItems | cost  |
+----------+------------+-------+
| "shoes," | 1          | 59.25 |
+----------+------------+-------+
1 row in set (0.279 secs)
```

How would you go about updating this record? Let's say you want to add another item like jeans. You could code this into a method similar to:

```
public static void addItem(Key key, String itemDescr, double cost) { ❶
    client.operate(null, key,
        Operation.append(new Bin("items", itemDescr+",")),
        Operation.add(new Bin("totalItems", 1)), ❷
        Operation.add(new Bin("cost", cost)) ❸


    );
}
```

This method does one call to the Aerospike client and one transaction on the database. This transaction contains three distinct operations:

❶ It appends a string onto an existing string, in this case the item description. If the "items" bin did not exist Aerospike would automatically create that bin.

❷ It adds one to the "totalItems" bin. Again, if the bin doesn't exist it will be created with a default value of zero and then have the passed value of one added.

❸ It adds the cost of the items to the running cost.

This method could be called to add two new items to the cart:

```
addItem(key, "jeans", 29.95);
addItem(key, "shirt", 19.95);
```

This would give you a database entry that looked like:

```
>aql> select * from test.cart;
+----------------------+------------+--------+
| items                | totalItems | cost   |
+----------------------+------------+--------+
| "shoes,jeans,shirt," | 3          | 109.15 |
+----------------------+------------+--------+
1 row in set (0.187 secs)
```

Simplifying the Program

Your program created an initial record with hardcoded bins. However, since Aerospike will automatically create bins that are missing, this step is actually not necessary. You can simplify your program by just using the addItem method. If the record already has items in it, the new item will be appended. If there are no items in the record or the record does not exist, Aerospike will create the record for you, automatically creating the items, totalItems, and cost bins.

So your program could become:

```
client = new AerospikeClient("172.17.0.2", 3000);
Key key = new Key("test", "cart", 1);
client.delete(null, key);
addItem(key, "shoes", 59.25);
addItem(key, "jeans", 29.95);
addItem(key, "shirt", 19.95);
```

Note the addition of the following line:

```
client.delete(null, key);
```

This line simply ensures the record does not exist before running the program. If you didn't do this and ran the program multiple times, you would keep adding the same items to the cart.

Let's double-check this through AQL after this change:

```
aql> select * from test.cart;
+----------------------+------------+--------+
| items                | totalItems | cost   |
+----------------------+------------+--------+
| "shoes,jeans,shirt," | 3          | 109.15 |
+----------------------+------------+--------+
1 row in set (0.187 secs)
```

The Operation Class

In the previous example, you saw that the arguments describing what work Aerospike should do on the record were on the Operation class. Let's take a look at the common methods on this class, as shown in Table 4-1.

Table 4-1. Common operations on the Operation class

Method	Use
add(Bin)	Increments the bin by the amount in the value of the passed Bin. If the bin does not exist, it is created with the passed value. If either the value is non-numeric or the existing value in the bin on the database is nonnumeric, an AerospikeException is thrown with a resultCode of ResultCode.BIN_TYPE_ERROR.
append(Bin)	Adds the passed string value to the end of the string in the passed Bin. If the bin does not exist, it is created with the passed value. If either the value is not a String or the existing value in the bin on the database is not a String, an AerospikeException is thrown with a resultCode of ResultCode.BIN_TYPE_ERROR.
get()	Returns the contents of all the bins in the record.
get(String)	Returns the contents of the named bin. Returns nothing if the named bin does not exist.
put(Bin)	Sets the content of the bin in the database to the passed value.

Return value of operate()

Notice that some of these methods (the get methods) return a value. So how do you get access to these values? Recall that the actual signature of operate() is:

```
public Record operate(WritePolicy policy, Key key, Operation ... operations);
```

The returned Record contains the values specified to be read. So let's say you want to change our addItem method to return the current cost of the items in the cart. You could simply add a get("cost") operation to the list of operations being executed:

```
public static double addItem(Key key, String itemDescr, double cost) {
    Record record = client.operate(null, key,
        Operation.append(new Bin("items", itemDescr+",")),
        Operation.add(new Bin("totalItems", 1)),
        Operation.add(new Bin("cost", cost)),
        Operation.get("cost")
    );
    return record.getDouble("cost");
}
```

Notice that this example changed the return type of the method to double, added the extra Operation at the end of the list, and returned the value of the bin "cost" by invoking getDouble("cost") on the returned record.

Similarly, you can do this in Python:

```python
my_operations = [
  {"op": aerospike.OPERATOR_APPEND, "bin": "items", "val": f"{item_desc},"},
  {"op": aerospike.OPERATOR_INCR, "bin": "totalItems", "val": 1},
  {"op": aerospike.OPERATOR_INCR, "bin": "cost", "val": cost},
  {"op": aerospike.OPERATOR_READ, "bin": "cost"},
]
(record, metadata, bins) = client.operate(key, my_operations)
```

Order of operations

The operations on a single record are applied to the record in the order they are specified to the `operate()` call. Aerospike guarantees that the operations are applied atomically and transactionally, so either all the operations happen or none of them, and no other thread can affect the record between the first operation and the last.

This order of operations can sometimes be important. For example, suppose you wanted Aerospike to return the cost of the items in the cart before you inserted the item and the cost after the item was inserted. You can modify the program to do this:

```java
Record record = client.operate(null, key,
        Operation.get("cost"),
        Operation.append(new Bin("items", itemDescr+",")),
        Operation.add(new Bin("totalItems", 1)),
        Operation.add(new Bin("cost", cost)),
        Operation.get("cost")
    );
```

Here you're getting the value of the `cost` bin before you update it, and again after you update it. This is valid in Aerospike, but what does it return? Thankfully the `Record` object has a useful `toString()` method, so you can inspect the returned values by adding the following straight after the `Record` is returned:

```java
System.out.println(record);
```

When you do this, you can see what is returned on subsequent calls. Here the same `operate` command is called three times:

```
(gen:1),(exp:0),(bins:(cost:59.25))
(gen:2),(exp:0),(bins:(cost:[59.25, 89.2]))
(gen:3),(exp:0),(bins:(cost:[89.2, 109.15]))
```

The first value returned is the generation count, that is, how many times this record has been modified. Then the expiry of the record if a TTL had been set, as detailed in the previous chapter. Finally, the bins are returned and you can see the `cost` bin is returned as a number on the first call, and as a list with two values on the two subsequent calls.

This makes sense when you think about it. On the first call, there was no `cost` bin, so Aerospike had nothing to return here. The `get("cost")` operation at the end of the list did have something to return, so Aerospike determined there was only one value to return for the `cost` bin, so it was returned as a single value. However, on subsequent calls, there was a valid value in the cost bin for both the `get("cost")` call at the start of the operation list and the one at the end of the list, so Aerospike has to return both values. It does this by wrapping both values in a list.

ListOperation and MapOperation

The operations you've seen so far have been fairly simple. A lot of the power of operations however comes from their ability to act on Aerospike's CDTs—lists and maps. These were briefly introduced in Chapter 2, but let's look at them in more detail.

Lists

A list is an ordered collection of elements. Like all CDTs in Aerospike, the elements can be of any supported type—including other lists and maps—and there is no requirement for the elements to be of a homogeneous type. So for example, a list might contain:

```
["sofa", 255.99, 2, ["black", "red", "white"]]
```

In this case the list contains a string (`sofa`), a double (`255.99`), a long (`2`), and a list.

Lists can be accessed in their entirety, or by index, value, or rank. To understand these concepts, let's look at an example. Consider the following list:

```
[1, 4, 7, 3, 9, 26, 11]
```

The index is the position of an element in the list starting with zero. The value is the value of the element identified by a specific index, and the rank is the index of an element in the list assuming the values are sorted. Table 4-2 shows the properties for this list.

Table 4-2. List properties for a sample list

	1	4	7	3	9	26	11
Value	1	4	7	3	9	26	11
Index	0 or −7	1 or −6	2 or −5	3 or −4	4 or −3	5 or −2	6 or −1
Rank	0 or −7	2 or −5	3 or −4	1 or −6	4 or −3	6 or −1	5 or −2

Note that both indexes and ranks can be specified with a negative value, with a negative meaning, "start at the end of the list and work backward." They also both start with zero for the first item.

The value and index are fairly self-explanatory, but let's look at how you arrived at a rank of 3 (or −4) for the value of "7." Remember that the rank is the value order after the list is sorted. So, sorting the list gives:

```
[1, 3, 4, 7, 9, 11, 26]
```

In this sorted list, the index (i.e., position in the list) of "7" is 3, or coming from the end of the list, −4. If you're confused as to why the "7" is position 3, remember that the first item in the list ("1") is index 0, so "3" is index 1, "4" is index 2, and "7" is index 3.

Let's take a look at a simple program to show how you would query these:

```java
public class ListMapExamples {
    private static final String LIST_BIN = "list";
    private static IAerospikeClient client
                    = new AerospikeClient("localhost", 3000);
    private static Key key = new Key("test", "sample", 1);

    private static void show(Operation operation, String description) {
        Record record = client.operate(null, key, operation);
        System.out.println(description + ": " + record.getValue(LIST_BIN));
    }

    public static void main(String[] args) {
        List<Integer> list = Arrays.asList(1, 4, 7, 3, 9, 26, 11);
        client.put(null, key, new Bin(LIST_BIN, list));

        show(ListOperation.getByIndex(LIST_BIN, 1, ListReturnType.VALUE),
            "Index of 1");
        show(ListOperation.getByRank(LIST_BIN, 1, ListReturnType.VALUE),
            "Rank of 1");
        show(ListOperation.getByValue(LIST_BIN, Value.get(1),
            ListReturnType.VALUE), "Value of 1");
        client.close();
    }
}
```

The output of this program reflects what was mentioned earlier for the index, rank, and value:

```
Index of 1: 4
Rank of 1: 3
Value of 1: [1]
```

Lists can be defined as ORDERED or UNORDERED. An UNORDERED list preserves the order of elements as they were inserted and is the default. An ORDERED list, however, will have the elements maintained in sorted order by Aerospike, irrespective of the order in which they were inserted. Since the lists are maintained in sorted order, in an ORDERED list the rank is the same as the index.

Maps

A map is a collection of items, each of which has a key and a value. Most programming languages have some variant of this called a map, a dictionary, or so on. The keys can be integers, strings, or blobs and the elements can be of any supported data type inside the Aerospike database.

It is necessary to ensure the client programming language supports the format of the map being used. For example, Node.js does not support integers as map keys, so reading such a map into the Node.js client will give errors, whereas it will work fine in other languages like Java.

Maps can be accessed by key, value, index, or rank. Again, this is best understood with an example. Consider the following map:

```
{a:1, b:2, c:30, y:30, z:26}
```

For this map, the properties in Table 4-3 apply.

Table 4-3. Map properties for a sample map

	a:1	b:2	c:30	y:30	z:26
Key	a	b	c	y	z
Value	1	2	30	30	26
Index	0 or −5	1 or −4	2 or −3	3 or −2	4 or −1
Rank	0 or −5	1 or −4	3 or −2	4 or −1	2 or −3

As can be seen in Table 4-3:

- The *key* is the identifier of the element in the map.
- The *value* is the value of the element identified by a specific map key.
- The *index* is the key order of the value in the map.
- The *rank* is the value order of the element in the map. If multiple elements have the same value (such as c:30 and y:30 in Table 4-3), their rank is based on the index order.

To give an example of when you might use these, consider a map that holds scores of people who have played a game. The keys of the map are the player IDs, and the values correspond to the score that player has. In this case:

- Retrieving a value by key will return the score for the passed player ID.
- To get the player with the highest score get the item with rank 0, and the player with the lowest score can be retrieved by getting the item with a rank of −1.
- The player with the lowest player ID can be retrieved using an index of 0, although this is not particularly useful in this example.

Maps can be UNORDERED, KEY_ORDERED, or KEY_VALUE_ORDERED. The API is the same for all map types, with Aerospike sorting the maps as needed. For example, if a map is stored as UNORDERED on the storage device and a call is made to get the element with the first index, Aerospike must retrieve the map off the storage device, sort the map, then return the element with the first index. For large maps, this sorting can consume significant CPU cycles. If the map had been stored as KEY_ORDERED, the map returned from the storage device would have already been sorted, allowing Aerospike to skip the sorting step.

KEY_ORDERED maps are the most useful with the maps stored on the storage device sorted by key. This makes operations on the keys very efficient as repeated key operations such as getByKeyRange() do not need to sort the map on each call.

Operations

Now that you understand the basic features of an Aerospike list and map, let's look at how you can use these. Both lists and maps are very powerful and, as you will see in Chapter 6, form the basis of many of the data modeling techniques you will use.

If you're getting confused between operate and operations, don't be!

- *Operations* tell the database what to do, that is, the actions to perform. There are multiple classes with static methods that create Operation instances, including Operation, MapOperation, and ListOperation.
- operate() is the API call that passes these actions to the database so that it can execute them.

Similar to the `Operation` class, there are also `ListOperation` and `MapOperation` classes that contain the respective operations. There are also other operation classes such as `HllOperation` that perform HyperLogLog operations, but that is beyond the scope of this book.

The shopping cart example you saw earlier in this chapter was good, but not great. The items were just a concatenated string, which makes manipulating it difficult; it's not very flexible. For example, maybe you want to store a reference to the original item so that if the cost changes when an item is in the cart it can be detected and a warning shown to the user.

To do this, you will turn each item in the example into a `map` and store these maps into a list of items in the shopping cart. You will then add some operations to the cart example.

First, let's define a method that will take the information for our item and turn it into a map:

```
public Map<String, Object> createItem(String itemDescr,
            double cost, String originalItem) {
    Map<String, Object> result = new HashMap<>();
    result.put("cost", cost);
    result.put("descr", itemDescr);
    result.put("orig", originalItem);
    return result;
}
```

Then, to insert an item, you can use a list operation:

```
public static void addItem(IAerospikeClient client, Key key,
            Map<String, Object> item) {
    client.operate(null, key, ListOperation.append("items", Value.get(item)));
}
```

In this method, you call `client.operate` again, this time passing in a `ListOperation` that appends the item to the end of the list. You will notice that the item is wrapped in a `Value.get(...)` call. This is a common pattern you will find in Aerospike, especially around `ListOperations` and `MapOperations`. Wrapping list and map operations allows Aerospike to specify a set of supported types that it understands without needing a large set of method overloads. Taking `Object` as a parameter without the wrapper would be too generic. The wrapper prevents compile-time checking of the passed values, and the `Value` wrappers also help the Aerospike client with serialization to send the information to the server.

Now you can insert a few items into the shopping cart list like this:

```
addItem(client, key, createItem("shoes", 59.25, "/items/item1234"));
addItem(client, key, createItem("jeans", 29.95, "/items/item2378"));
addItem(client, key, createItem("shirt", 19.95, "/items/item88293"));
```

Inspecting the output in AQL shows you the new nested structures:

```
aql> select * from test.cart;
+-----------------------------------------------------------------------
| items
+-----------------------------------------------------------------------
| LIST('[{"cost":59.25, "descr":"shoes", "orig":"/items/item1234"}, {"cost"
+-----------------------------------------------------------------------
1 row in set (0.510 secs)
```

Note that the actual output is far longer than shown here and has been truncated for ease of reading. However, this does present a common problem. As records become larger and more complex, examining them becomes increasingly difficult. Luckily, AQL supports various display modes, as shown in Table 4-4.

Table 4-4. Display modes for AQL

AQL mode	Output
TABLE	Shows the output in a textual table. This works well for small results, but larger results get truncated and so don't display well. This is the default.
JSON	Shows the output formatted in JSON. Note that JSON does not support keys that are not strings so if a bin contains a map that has integer keys, for example, these entries will not be displayed.
RAW	Shows the full output of each bin, one bin per line. The output is not truncated, so if the records contain megabytes of data, for example, a lot of data will be output.

The one that makes the most sense here is JSON:

```
aql> set output json
OUTPUT = JSON
aql> select * from test.cart;
[
  [
    {
      "items": [
        {
          "cost": 59.25,
          "descr": "shoes",
          "orig": "/items/item1234"
        },
        {
          "cost": 29.949999999999999,
          "descr": "jeans",
          "orig": "/items/item2378"
        },
```

```json
        {
            "cost": 19.949999999999999,
            "descr": "shirt",
            "orig": "/items/item88293"
        }
    ]
}
],
[
    {
        "Status": 0
    }
]
]
```

You can see that our cart now comprises a list with three elements, each of which is a map.

Naturally, you can also combine multiple operations into a single API call. For example, let's say you want to remove the second item in the list and return the number of items remaining in the list. You could do this as follows:

```
Record record = client.operate(null, key,
        ListOperation.removeByIndex("items", index, ListReturnType.NONE),
        ListOperation.size("items"));
Int remaining = record.getInt("items");
```

In our case, this will result in `remaining` having a value of 2. As before, the operations are applied in order, so the count is taken after the item has been removed.

Did you notice when you invoked the `ListOperation.removeByIndex` call, you passed a parameter of `ListReturnType.NONE`? This determines what Aerospike returns from this call. `NONE` obviously specifies no return value, but there are other things you could return. For example, if you passed `ListReturnType.VALUE` here, the removed item would be returned; `ListReturnType.COUNT` would return the number of elements removed.

There are other API calls that look similar. For example, to remove two items from the list starting from the passed index you can use `removeByIndexRange`:

```
Record record = client.operate(null, key,
        ListOperation.removeByIndex("items", index, 2 ListReturnType.NONE));
int removed = record.getInt("items");
```

Inverted Flag

All the return values for the `ListReturnType` flag, and the corresponding `MapReturn Type` flag, are discrete—only one can be specified—with the exception of `ListReturn Type.INVERTED`. This flag can be specified with any of the other return types and effectively inverts the meaning of the list command.

If you were to add this flag to the preceding operation, our code would become:

```
Record record = client.operate(null, key,
    ListOperation.removeByIndex("items", index,
        ListReturnType.NONE | ListReturnType.INVERTED));
int removed = record.getInt("items");
```

The presence of the INVERTED flag tells Aerospike to remove all items in the list *except* the item at the passed index. So if you started with 5 elements in the list or 50, you would still end up with a list containing just 1 element.

Contexts

List and map operations can be nested to any arbitrary depth. In our cart example, you have maps inside a list, so a nesting depth of two. This presents a problem when using list and map operations: how to affect an item that is not at the top level?

The answer is that all of these APIs take a *context* parameter. This context describes the path from the top level down to the specific list or map you wish to affect. In Java this is a varargs parameter to the list or map operation and, as such, goes at the end of each call. For example, let's say you wanted to set the price of our "shoes" item to be $49 instead of $59.25. You know that this is the first item in the list, so you would use this MapOperation:

```
client.operate(null, key,
    MapOperation.put(MapPolicy.Default, "items", Value.get("cost"),
        Value.get(49), CTX.listIndex(0)));
```

Let's look at what this call is doing. The first parameter to the MapOperation is the MapPolicy. In this case you're just using Default, which tells Aerospike to use an UNORDERED map. If you preferred to use a KEY_ORDERED map, you could have specified this here. The next parameter is the bin name ("items"), which in a production system would obviously be extracted to a constant. Following this is the map key you want to set ("cost"), then the value you want to set it to (49), both wrapped in a Value.get(...) call. Finally comes the context (CTX.listIndex(0)), which says to Aerospike, "the map on which I want this value set can be found as the first element in the list."

Note that the type of the item you want to affect is a *map*, so you have to use a MapOperation even though the map is contained within a list. The path down to that map from the top (bin level) is shown through the context. This probably would make more sense if the context were the first parameter rather than the last, but sadly in Java varargs must be the last parameter.

You can find more list and map operations in your client driver documentation on the Aerospike website along with performance complexity estimations under the List (*https://oreil.ly/X3NJz*) and Map (*https://oreil.ly/1wblN*) expands in the navigation menu. The Aerospike website lists these functions in their C implementation, so your specific driver invocation may vary.

Expressions

One very powerful feature of Aerospike is the ability to use expressions. An expression can be used to filter whether to perform a particular operation on a record, compute values on the fly, write derived quantities to a record, and so on. Let's take a look at some of these.

Filter Expressions

Filter expressions allow operations to be performed on the server only if the particular filter expression returns true. So, for example, let's say you want to update the state of an order to be COMPLETED, but only if the current state is PROCESSING. You could achieve this by reading the record, ensuring that the current state is PROCESSING, and then updating the state, but another thread might have changed the record state between when you read it and when you want to write it, causing us to have to use check-and-set semantics as discussed in Chapter 3.

A better way would be to use an expression on the put operation to create a conditional write. The expression is evaluated as part of the put transaction on the server, meaning that it is atomic and cannot be interrupted by another thread.

Let's assume that our cart has a state on it, for example, by using:

```
client.put(null, key, new Bin("state", "PROCESSING"));
```

Now, just update the state using:

```
client.put(null, key, new Bin("state", "COMPLETED"));
```

This will blindly overwrite the existing state without performing a check first. So you have to augment this with a filter expression.

Filter expressions are specified on the Policy of the operation. In this case you're performing a write operation, so you need to create a WritePolicy and pass this to the operation. In this case, you would pass something similar to:

```
WritePolicy wp = new WritePolicy(client.getWritePolicyDefault());
wp.filterExp =
    Exp.build(Exp.eq(Exp.stringBin("state"), Exp.val("PROCESSING")));
client.put(wp, key, new Bin("state", "COMPLETED"));
```

Here you have created a new `WritePolicy` based on the existing write policy defaults and then set the filter expression. The expression itself is written in prefix (or Polish) notation, with the operation coming first then the arguments. So in this case, the expression that does the work is really:

```
Exp.eq(Exp.stringBin("state"), Exp.val("PROCESSING"))
```

`Exp.eq` compares two expressions for equality and returns a Boolean expression. `Exp.stringBin("state")` reads a bin called `"state"`, which should be a string value, and `Exp.val("PROCESSING")` forms a constant expression holding the string value `"PROCESSING"`. The upshot of this is that the expression will return true if the bin `"state"` contains `"PROCESSING"`. In infix notation, this would be:

```
stringBin("state") == "PROCESSING"
```

There are lots of different expressions that you can use to manipulate the record's data into the expression that you want. There are comparison operators like `Exp.eq` you saw in the preceding, arithmetic operators like `Exp.add`, logical operators like `Exp.and`, control operations like `Exp.cond`, which acts as an if-then-else statement, and so on. Additionally, other classes like `ListExp` and `MapExp` allow manipulation of lists and maps respectively, similar to the `ListOperation` and `MapOperation` you saw earlier. A full coverage of expressions is beyond the scope of this book, but you can find details on them in the Aerospike documentation (*https://oreil.ly/WKo_p*).

We will touch on just a few more very useful features of expressions before we wrap up our coverage of them.

Trilean Logic

Most programmers are familiar with Boolean logic, which allows only two values, true and false. There are rules that govern the behavior of Boolean logic, such as "false AND anything equals false." In Aerospike expressions, you use trilean logic, which has three values: true, false, and *unknown*.

Why is this necessary? Well, in Aerospike's architecture there are typically two main components of a record—the metadata and the data. The metadata is typically kept in memory for efficiency, whereas the data is typically persisted on flash storage. This makes metadata access significantly faster than data access, so if you can determine if an expression is either true or false based just on metadata, you can potentially skip loading the record from storage.

Consider an expression that needs to determine if the bin `"state"` in the record is `PROCESSING` and if the last update to the record was within the last day. You saw how to check the bin data in the preceding example, so you will build on this by adding the last update time (LUT).

In pseudocode, what you want is:

```
stringBin("state") == "PROCESSING" AND lastUpdateTime <= 1day
```

The expressions have a handy `sinceUpdate()` expression you can use to get the time since the record was updated in milliseconds. You can use Java's `TimeUnits` to get the number of milliseconds in a day, so you would end up with:

```
Exp.and(
    Exp.eq(Exp.stringBin("state"), Exp.val("PROCESSING")),
    Exp.le(Exp.sinceUpdate(), Exp.val(TimeUnit.DAYS.toMillis(1))
}
```

Aerospike keeps the LUT in the metadata but the `state` bin of the record could be stored on a storage device. To evaluate this, Aerospike would apply a first pass to the expression, evaluating all the metadata first and treating bin data as `UNKNOWN`. If the resulting value is `true` or `false` the expression is matched or not matched. However, if it's `UNKNOWN` the data is loaded off storage and the result reevaluated, which will return `true` or `false`.

As an example of this, let's consider the preceding expression on a record updated a week ago. The first part of the expression (`Exp.eq(Exp.stringBin("state")`, `Exp.val("PROCESSING")`)) requires data to be loaded off storage and cannot be evaluated at this time, so it returns `UNKNOWN`. However, the second part of the expression (`Exp.le(Exp.sinceUpdate(), Exp.val(TimeUnit.DAYS.toMillis(1)))`) can be evaluated using only metadata and returns `false` as the record was last updated a week ago. `false` and anything (including `UNKNOWN`) is `false`, so the code can fail the expression without loading the data from a storage device.

Contrast this to a record that was last updated six hours ago. In this case the first expression clause still returns `UNKNOWN`, but the second clause returns `true`. `UNKNOWN` and `true` is `UNKNOWN`, so the first pass returns `UNKNOWN`. The data is then loaded off storage and the expression reevaluated. The expression can be definitively evaluated, based on the contents of the `state` bin.

Read Expressions

Sometimes it is useful to return data that is derived from the contents of a record but does not actually exist in the record. These expressions cannot be used as filter expressions as they do not return a Boolean value but rather serve to return data to the client.

For example, let's consider a use case where you have the total cost of items in the cart stored and you want to return the average cost. You also have a list of the items, so you can derive the average cost from these two pieces of information.

First, you will change your `addItem` method to keep a running sum of the cost:

```
public static void addItem(IAerospikeClient client, Key key,
        Map<String, Object> item) {

    client.operate(null, key, ListOperation.append("items", Value.get(item)),
                Operation.add(new Bin("total", (double)item.get("cost"))));
}
```

Now, when you add your items you will have a total cost:

```
addItem(client, key, addItem("shoes", 59.25, "/items/item1234"));
addItem(client, key, addItem("jeans", 29.95, "/items/item2378"));
addItem(client, key, addItem("shirt", 19.95, "/items/item88293"));
```

This can be shown through AQL:

```
aql> select total from test.cart where pk = 1;
---------+----+
| total  | PK |
+--------+----+
| 109.15 | 1  |
+--------+----+
1 row in set (0.000 secs)
```

Now let's add a method that will use a read expression to get the average price back by dividing the total bin by the size of the list:

```
public static double getAverageCost(IAerospikeClient client, Key key) {
    Record record = client.operate(null, key,
        ExpOperation.read("avg", Exp.build(
            Exp.div(
                Exp.floatBin("total"),
                Exp.toFloat(ListExp.size(Exp.listBin("items")))
            )
        ), ExpReadFlags.DEFAULT));
    return record.getDouble("avg");
    }
}
```

There are a number of things to unpack here! Let's take a closer look. The `operate()` command should be familiar to you by now, but you're using a new sort of operation here, an `ExpOperation` (short for expression operation). This has two variants: `read` and `write`. `read` is used to return values back to the client and `write` is used to update values in the record itself. Here you're using a `read`.

Given the purpose of a `read` operation is to return information to the client, and that `"avg"` doesn't exist as a bin in the record, you need to tell the operation how to return the data. This is the `avg` parameter in the call, saying, "create a pseudo-bin in the returned information called `avg`." The value of this field will be the result of the expression, which in this case is the value in the bin `"total"` divided by the number of items in the list `"items"`.

Note that the size of the list is an integer type and you cannot validly divide a float by an integer; hence you had to cast the list size to a float using `Exp.toFloat`. The other interesting thing to note is that the `ListExp.size(...)` function takes a list. This is typically a bin containing a list as in the example here:

```
ListExp.size(Exp.listBin("items"))
```

However, some of the list operations such as `getByIndexRange(...)` return a list, and this can be used as the argument to `ListExp.size(...)` and other operations. This effectively allows you to "chain" operations together. For example:

```
ListExp.size(
    ListExp.append(ListPolicy.Default, Exp.val(10), Exp.listBin("items")
)
```

This will append 10 onto the list in bin `"items"` and then return the size of the list.

It should be noted that this expression is not perfect. If there are no items in the list, `ListExp.size(...)` will return zero, and hence you will be dividing by zero, which will cause Aerospike to throw an exception. Instead of having an exception thrown, it would be better to just show the average as $0.00.

There are a couple of ways of solving this, the easiest of which is telling Aerospike to ignore errors. You can do this by changing the flags you pass to the `ExpOpera tion.read(...)` method to include `ExpReadFlags.EVAL_NO_FAIL`. Note that only expression execution exceptions are trapped with this flag. Other issues, such as the server falling over in the middle of processing the operation, will still throw exceptions.

So instead of:

```
Record record = client.operate(null, key,
    ExpOperation.read("avg", Exp.build(
        Exp.div(
            Exp.floatBin("total"),
            Exp.toFloat(ListExp.size(Exp.listBin("items")))
        )
    ), ExpReadFlags.DEFAULT));
```

You can use:

```
Record record = client.operate(null, key,
    ExpOperation.read("avg", Exp.build(
        Exp.div(
            Exp.floatBin("total"),
            Exp.toFloat(ListExp.size(Exp.listBin("items")))
        )
    ), ExpReadFlags.DEFAULT | ExpReadFlags.EVAL_NO_FAIL));
```

In this case, Aerospike will catch the exception silently and the avg bin in the result set will be null. When you get null as an integer, Aerospike returns 0, which is exactly what you're after.

Batch Operations

Batch read operations were covered in Chapter 3. As a reminder, a batch read will take an array of keys and return an array of records identified by those keys. If a record is not found, null will be returned for that key instead.

Using Batch Operations

Batch reads allow you to read many records in a single database call, reducing networking chatter, code complexity, and latency. This can be attractive to use for every call, but you must be aware of some common pitfalls with using batch read operations:

- There is some overhead on both the client and server when starting a batch operation. For small batch sizes this can create significant overhead. The worst case is doing a batch operation with just one record, which is substantially slower than doing a straight key-value read.

- The server-side batch architecture has a set of cached, reusable 128 kiB buffers for returning records to the client. If a single record in a batch is larger than this size, a temporary buffer must be allocated for that record and then discarded at the end of the batch call, resulting in lower performance than using records less than this limit due to constant memory allocation and deallocation. These allocations can be tracked by monitoring the batch_index_huge_buffers metric. See Chapter 8 for more details on monitoring.

- Batch operations can request a lot of data from the database, which can cause the batch response from Aerospike to slow down and wait using EWOULDBLOCK. You can monitor for this from the Aerospike server's batch_index_delay metric.

Batch reads are probably the most useful; however, Aerospike's batch capabilities extend beyond this. Batches in Aerospike are very efficient—the Aerospike client will work out which keys belong to which server and send all the keys to the appropriate server in one network packet. Depending on the settings in the BatchPolicy, the servers may be sent the keys they need to process in parallel, allowing them to stream the results back to the client in parallel.

Let's look at a couple of other uses for batches.

Batch Writes

Sometimes it's useful to perform the same set of operations across multiple records. These can be writes, appends, list or map operations, and so on. A batch write fulfills this need, taking an array of keys and the operations that should be applied to the records identified by those keys and efficiently performing the operation on them. For a rather contrived example, consider a set that holds records of people, including the state and the tax rate for that state:

```
aql> select * from test.people
+----+----------+-----+-------+---------+
| PK | name     | age | state | taxRate |
+----+----------+-----+-------+---------+
| 5  | "Alex"   | 72  | "FL"  | 1.15    |
| 6  | "Lou"    | 25  | "CA"  | 2.05    |
| 0  | "Tim"    | 312 | "CO"  | 1.35    |
| 7  | "Jill"   | 44  | "IA"  | 0.44    |
| 2  | "Sue"    | 43  | "FL"  | 1.15    |
| 8  | "Manish" | 49  | "CO"  | 1.35    |
| 4  | "Mary"   | 33  | "NV"  | 0.95    |
| 1  | "Albert" | 29  | "CO"  | 1.35    |
| 9  | "Sunil"  | 54  | "CA"  | 2.05    |
| 3  | "Joe"    | 19  | "GA"  | 1.25    |
+----+----------+-----+-------+---------+
10 rows in set (0.148 secs)
```

Imagine the use case called for increasing the tax rate of these 10 people by 0.02%. You have all the information needed to form the keys of the records you need to update, so let's do that first:

```
Key[] keys = new Key[10];
for (int i = 0; i < 10; i++) {
    keys[i] = new Key("test", "people", i);
}
```

Now all you have to do is tell Aerospike to go and update the tax rate of these people. As the operation that needs to be applied to each record is the same, a batch write is perfect for this.

The line you need is:

```
client.operate(null, null, keys, Operation.add(new Bin("taxRate", 0.02)));
```

This operate overload takes four parameters. The first is the BatchPolicy, a class that is common between all the batch overloads including batch reads and batch writes. Hence it contains general information such as network timeouts, number of retries, and so on. It does not contain anything specific to writing the information. That's the job of the second parameter, a BatchWritePolicy. This contains information specific to how you want the writes to behave, such as what to do if the record does not exist. You are not using any special policies here, so passing null for both parameters is fine. Following this is the array of keys, then the operations you want to perform on each record, which is just increasing the tax rate by a fixed amount.

After running this code, you can see the results using AQL again:

```
aql> select * from test.people
+----+----------+-----+-------+---------+
| PK | name     | age | state | taxRate |
+----+----------+-----+-------+---------+
| 2  | "Sue"    | 43  | "FL"  | 1.17    |
| 0  | "Tim"    | 312 | "CO"  | 1.37    |
| 4  | "Mary"   | 33  | "NV"  | 0.97    |
| 1  | "Albert" | 29  | "CO"  | 1.37    |
| 9  | "Sunil"  | 54  | "CA"  | 2.07    |
| 7  | "Jill"   | 44  | "IA"  | 0.46    |
| 8  | "Manish" | 49  | "CO"  | 1.37    |
| 5  | "Alex"   | 72  | "FL"  | 1.17    |
| 6  | "Lou"    | 25  | "CA"  | 2.07    |
| 3  | "Joe"    | 19  | "GA"  | 1.27    |
+----+----------+-----+-------+---------+
10 rows in set (0.166 secs)
```

You can see that the tax rate has increased across all the people in this set.

Note that if you put a filter expression onto a batch operation, the filter applies to each record. For example, let's say that instead of increasing everyone's tax rate by 0.02%, you only want to apply that operation to those people who live in Colorado (CO). You need to create a filter expression that matches these criteria:

```
Expression exp = Exp.build(Exp.eq(Exp.stringBin("state"), Exp.val("CO")));
```

The expression will return true when the string in bin "state" is "CO". You now need to apply this to the filterExp on the policy. But if you look closely at the API you will see that both BatchPolicy and BatchWritePolicy take a filterExp! Which one should you use?

In this instance, you can use either. If both are specified, the more specific one (i.e., the one on the BatchWritePolicy) will override the one on the BatchPolicy. There are very few cases where it makes sense to specify both filterExps, so just be aware that it normally doesn't make a difference. For this example, you can set it on the BatchWritePolicy:

```
BatchWritePolicy bwp = new BatchWritePolicy();
Expression exp = Exp.build(Exp.eq(Exp.stringBin("state"), Exp.val("CO")));
bwp.filterExp = exp;
client.operate(null, bwp, keys, Operation.add(new Bin("taxRate", 0.02)));
```

Arbitrary Batch Operations

Sometimes there is a set of operations that needs to happen to several records, but the operations are different for different records. For example, consider the data from the previous example:

```
aql> select * from test.people
+----+----------+-----+-------+---------+
| PK | name     | age | state | taxRate |
+----+----------+-----+-------+---------+
| 5  | "Alex"   | 72  | "FL"  | 1.15    |
| 6  | "Lou"    | 25  | "CA"  | 2.05    |
| 0  | "Tim"    | 312 | "CO"  | 1.35    |
| 7  | "Jill"   | 44  | "IA"  | 0.44    |
| 2  | "Sue"    | 43  | "FL"  | 1.15    |
| 8  | "Manish" | 49  | "CO"  | 1.35    |
| 4  | "Mary"   | 33  | "NV"  | 0.95    |
| 1  | "Albert" | 29  | "CO"  | 1.35    |
| 9  | "Sunil"  | 54  | "CA"  | 2.05    |
| 3  | "Joe"    | 19  | "GA"  | 1.25    |
+----+----------+-----+-------+---------+
10 rows in set (0.148 secs)
```

Let's say you want to add one to Joe's age, change Sue's state to Ohio (OH), decrease Mary's tax rate by 0.1%, read Jill's age and tax rate, delete Alex's record, and change Tim's name to Timothy. You could do this in several separate calls to the client, but you could just use an arbitrary batch operation. Let's see what this would look like:

```
aKey joesKey = new Key("test", "people", 3);
Key suesKey = new Key("test", "people", 2);
Key marysKey = new Key("test", "people", 4);
Key jillsKey = new Key("test", "people", 7);
Key alexsKey = new Key("test", "people", 5);
Key timsKey = new Key("test", "people", 0);
Operation[] joesOps = new Operation[] {Operation.add(new Bin("age", 1))};
Operation[] suesOps = new Operation[] {Operation.put(new Bin("state", "OH"))};
Operation[] marysOps = new Operation[] {Operation.add(new Bin("taxRate", -0.1))};
Operation[] timsOps = new Operation[] {Operation.put(new Bin("name",
"Timothy"))};
BatchRead jillsRead = new BatchRead(jillsKey, new String[] {"age", "taxRate"});
client.operate(null, Arrays.asList(
        new BatchWrite(joesKey, joesOps),
        new BatchWrite(suesKey, suesOps),
        new BatchWrite(marysKey, marysOperations),
        jillsRead,
        new BatchDelete(alexsKey),
        new BatchWrite(timsKey, timsOps)
        ));
System.out.println(jillsRead.record);
```

The code is really broken into three parts. The first is just defining the keys for the various people, and the second is defining the operations for the BatchWrites. Each of the BatchWrites takes an array of operations, although you're just using one operation per record.

The last and most important part is the actual call to operate(). This just takes a BatchPolicy and a list of BatchRecords. BatchRecord is a superclass of BatchRead, BatchWrite, BatchDelete, and so on.

Most of the BatchRecords you're using do not need to return a result, so you can just instantiate the appropriate operation within the operate() call. The exception is the BatchRead, where you read Jill's age and tax rate. The results for all operations are returned in the BatchRecord passed to the operation, so you need to save Jill's BatchRead in a variable. When the call succeeds, you can get the information you need from the .record part of the BatchRecord.

Secondary Indexes

Similar to many other databases, Aerospike has secondary indexes that allow for efficient querying of records that match specific criteria, for example, "show me all the people who live in Colorado" or "get all people between ages 25 and 39." Secondary indexes are defined on a bin in a particular set and must have a type, such as numeric or string. Table 4-5 shows the different types of secondary indexes that are supported and the operations available on them.

Table 4-5. Secondary index types

Type	Allowed operations	Comments
NUMERIC	Equality, range comparisons	For indexing and querying integer type bins. Includes long, shorts, etc.; however, floating-point types (float, double) are not supported.
STRING	Equality only	Aerospike stores a hash of the string to conserve space; hence only exact matches are supported. Strings are always case-sensitive comparisons.
GEO JSON	Point-in-region, region-contains-points	GeoJSON queries are an advanced topic not covered in this book but allow efficient comparisons of geospatial data.

Note that if a record contains a bin that has a secondary index defined on it, but the type in that bin does not match the secondary index type, that record will not be returned from a secondary index query. For example, consider a numeric index that is defined on a bin "age", but one record contains a string "40". This record will never match the secondary index.

To create secondary indexes you will use the Aerospike Administration tool, asadm. System administrators use this tool extensively to monitor and affect the Aerospike cluster. We will touch on it here, but it will be covered more fully in Chapter 7.

To start asadm, run:

```
% asadm [-h <ip_address>]
```

Like Aerospike's other tools, the IP address defaults to localhost (127.0.0.1), so for many local installations no parameter is needed after the command name.

This will place you in an interactive shell:

```
Admin>
```

Commands entered will have their results shown in real time. A good place to get started is entering **help** at this prompt. It will show a list of available commands. The shell supports help commands (see Chapter 7 for more details), as well as command completion, so if you know part of what you want to do you can type that in and then double-tap the Tab key to see what options are available.

First, you want to show what indexes there are:

```
Admin> show sindex
Admin>
```

You will find sindex used frequently in Aerospike documentation and tools as shorthand for "secondary index." In your environment, at the moment, there are no secondary indexes, so you need to create one.

asadm has two modes: *user mode* and *privileged mode*. User mode enables the viewing of information but does not allow cluster management such as creating secondary indexes. You need to change to privileged mode, which simply requires entering enable. In a production environment, only users with sufficient permissions are able to enter privileged mode, but you have not enabled security on your cluster yet, so you don't need to worry about this.

```
Admin> enable
Admin+>
```

Note the cursor changes slightly with the addition of the +, and the font will change to red.

Once in privileged mode you can create the index:

```
Admin+> manage sindex create numeric age_idx ns test set people bin age;
Use 'show sindex' to confirm age_idx was created successfully.

Admin+> show sindex
~~~Secondary Indexes (2023-08-28 13:00:08 UTC)~~~~
Index  |Namespace|   Set|Bin|    Bin|  Index|State
Name   |         |      |   |   Type|   Type|
age_idx|test     |people|age|numeric|default|RW
Number of rows: 1
```

You create the secondary index with the `manage sindex` command. Although it looks daunting at first glance, it is fairly readable and says the following: manage secondary indexes (`manage sindex`) and create a numeric index called `age_idx` (`create numeric age_idx`) in the namespace `test` (`ns test`) on the set `person` (`set person`) and the bin `age` (`bin age`). Remembering what parameters are needed is made much easier with the help system. To work out the parameters of the preceding command, do this:

```
Admin+> manage sindex help
"manage sindex" is used to create and delete secondary indexes. It should
be used in conjunction with the "show sindex" or "info sindex" command.
- create:
Usage: create <bin-type> <index-name> ns <ns> [set <set>] bin <bin-name> [in
<index-type>] [ctx <ctx-item> [. . .]]
bin-type - The bin type of the provided <bin-name>. Should be one of the
following values:
```

Note that the output has been truncated for the sake of brevity, but you can see the usage parameters. You can omit the last two parameters as these are used for indexing into CDTs.

Using the Secondary Index

Now that you have your secondary index, let's use it to query people in your set within a particular age range:

```
Statement stmt = new Statement();
stmt.setFilter(Filter.range("age", 25, 39));
stmt.setNamespace("test");
stmt.setSetName("people");
RecordSet recordSet = client.query(null, stmt);
while (recordSet.next()) {
    System.out.println(recordSet.getRecord());
}
recordSet.close();
```

The first thing you have to do is create a `Statement` object. This contains the parameters for the statement, including which namespace and set to run the query on. You specify the filter you want to use, in this case a range filter on the "age" bins with a minimum age of 25 and a maximum age of 39. Both ends of the range are inclusive, so it will pick up anyone aged 25 and 39 as well as people whose ages are in the middle of the range.

The query is then executed and returns a `RecordSet`. The `RecordSet` allows easy iteration through the matching records as shown here, with both the record and the key available once `next()` has returned true.

While this query looks innocuous, Aerospike does a lot of work behind the scenes for such a query. Imagine your Aerospike cluster contains a billion records in the people set with a million of these matching our criteria. Aerospike will, by default, fire a request off to each of the nodes in parallel. Each Aerospike server consults a memory tree that contains the value of the age bin for each record in the set. When matching records are found, they are streamed back to the client. This is known as a "scatter gather" algorithm due to scattering the request to all nodes and gathering the results back together at the client.

The client receives the responses from all nodes in parallel. It buffers some of them, but for large result sets it will rely on being able to pull more from the appropriate node(s) as needed rather than trying to store everything in memory. The client also keeps track of which records it has processed from which nodes, so if the query is interrupted by a node going down, for example, the client can continue to serve records from the cluster without needing to restart the query.

It is important to close the result set once you've finished processing it. This will free up client-side and server-side resources.

Multiple Predicate Queries

Aerospike only supports using one secondary index per query. So even if you had, say, an index defined on the "age" bin and a different index defined on the "state" bin and you wanted to find everyone between 25 and 39 in Colorado, you would only be able to use one of the indexes, not both. Typically, you would use the index with the highest selectivity in this case, that is, the one that would likely return the smallest set of responses.

However, there is an easy solution for handling multiple predicates like this. If you guessed "using expressions," you are correct! You can put an Expression on a query with a secondary index. When you do this, Aerospike will use the secondary index to load the records that match and then apply the Expression to each of those records, returning only the records that match the expression. So, to retrieve only the people between 25 and 39 in the state of Colorado (CO), you would change the code to the following:

```
Statement stmt = new Statement();
stmt.setFilter(Filter.range("age", 25, 39));
stmt.setNamespace("test");
stmt.setSetName("people");
QueryPolicy qp = new QueryPolicy(client.getQueryPolicyDefault()); ❹
qp.filterExp = Exp.build(Exp.eq(Exp.stringBin("state"), Exp.val("CO"))); ❺
RecordSet recordSet = client.query(qp, stmt); ❻
while (recordSet.next()) {
    System.out.println(recordSet.getRecord());
}
recordSet.close();
```

❹ Create a new `QueryPolicy` based on the default one.

❺ Set the `filterExp` value to the filter expression you want to use.

❻ Include the `QueryPolicy` instance in the `client.query` call.

Summary

In this chapter you looked at some of the more powerful features of Aerospike. The use of lists and maps adds a lot of depth to the capabilities of Aerospike and will feature heavily in the discussion of data modeling in Chapter 6. Expressions allow advanced filtering operations, while batches and secondary indexes allow bulk querying of records from Aerospike. The next chapter will focus on the architecture of Aerospike for a complete understanding of why it is so efficient.

CHAPTER 5

Architecture

Since you are just starting to use Aerospike, this chapter will not explain how the database is built. However, knowing some key aspects of how Aerospike works under the covers will help you understand why you do certain things with it and how to get the most out of its capabilities.

This chapter focuses on three major topics—scale out (horizontal scaling), scale up (vertical scaling), and how transaction management with strong consistency is accomplished on this distributed system.

Scale Out

To linearly scale performance latency and throughput, Aerospike must scale out on multiple commodity computers, aka nodes. To do this, Aerospike has several fundamental principles built into its heart. These foundational pillars affect how everything works in the database. The key goal of the scale-out architecture is to maintain a uniform distribution of data across data partitions and across nodes. Combined with the ability to support elasticity using dynamic addition and removal of nodes, this architecture ensures that the system avoids hot spots (overworked nodes or network connections) while providing excellent performance (both high throughput *and* extremely low latency) with linear scalability.

Shared-Nothing Database Cluster

Aerospike is a shared-nothing database, meaning that each node in a cluster does not share anything with the other nodes. The database cluster consists of a set of commodity server nodes, each of which has CPUs, memory (RAM), rotational disks (HDDs), and optional flash storage units (SSDs). These nodes are connected to each other using a standard TCP/IP network.

Several fundamental aspects of the database make it shared-nothing:

Every node is identical to every other node
> This is true in terms of both hardware capabilities and software. There are no master nodes and therefore no single points of failure.

Data-to-node mapping is on every node
> This means that there is always only one hop from the smart client direct to the data, with no intermediary steps required.

Data partitioning is done with distributed hash tables
> Aerospike uses an extremely random cryptographic hash on every key to spread data evenly across the cluster.

Long-running tasks and short tasks are prioritized in real time
> The database dynamically and intelligently handles the interplay between long-running tasks like rebalancing data when node count changes and short-running, low-latency tasks like transactions. This protects the SLAs on the short tasks.

Cluster management is dynamic
> Nodes can be added or dropped without interrupting transactions. Data rebalancing is done dynamically, and maintenance actions such as rolling upgrades happen without interrupting the service.

The basic idea behind all of these is to ensure that the cluster runs without operator intervention in the presence of dynamic node arrivals and departures, the data is uniformly distributed across nodes in the cluster, and the system delivers high performance and scales linearly as more client and server nodes are added to the system.

As shown in Figure 5-1, the Aerospike application architecture has two layers that communicate with the two layers in the client. These layers are:

Application layer
> Client application that requires a database

Client layer
> Aerospike API library implementation that is embedded inside the application

Distribution layer in Aerospike
> Intracluster communication

Data layer in Aerospike
> Interface to storage (both in-memory and persistent storage such as SSDs)

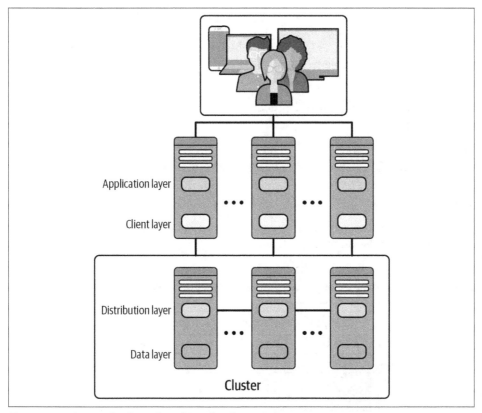

Figure 5-1. Aerospike shared-nothing database architecture

Data Distribution

A key aspect of Aerospike is its ability to divide and conquer the problem of high-scale datasets using a deterministic uniform distribution of data to minimize data migrations.

 Aerospike splits partitions using the digest of the RIPEMD-160 algorithm (*https://oreil.ly/O0tvh*) for hashing. The digest is the 20-byte hash value generated by applying the RIPEMD algorithm on the key. This algorithm is very robust against collisions. The distribution of keys in the digest space and therefore in the partition space is always uniform because even if the hash is skewed, the digest of it won't be.

A partition is the primary unit of data segmentation. The random cryptographic hash on every key spreads data evenly across nodes as shown in Figure 5-2. The hash splits data into 4,096 partitions to then be mapped to nodes in the cluster. The partition assignment algorithm objectives are:

Be deterministic
    Each node in the distributed system can independently compute the same partition map.

Distribute data uniformly
    Distribute master partitions and replica partitions across all nodes in the cluster equally.

Minimize data migrations
    When the cluster changes, with new nodes added or removed, the less data that must be moved around, the better.

Aerospike uses an algorithm that automatically creates uniform partition balancing across nodes while minimizing data migrations, as much as possible.

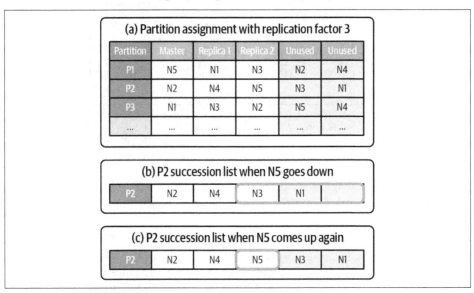

Figure 5-2. Partition map: partition to node assignment

Figure 5-2a shows the *partition map* for the data assignment on a five-node cluster with a replication factor of 3. Only the number of columns equal to the replication factor are used to show where data is mapped, the first three columns in the example shown.

The last two columns in the map are not the locations of data since the data is only replicated three times. Instead, the next columns store the rest of the nodes in the *succession list* of locations that data will be migrated to in case one of the nodes that has data on it fails.

Figure 5-2b shows what happens to the data in partition 2 if a node goes down or network connection to it is lost. In this example, node N5 goes down. Since the partition map already stores the information on where data will go next for that partition, the data is migrated to node N3, the next node listed in the map in the column to the right.

Note that this also shifts the next column to the left, so if node N3 were to also go down, node N1 would be next to receive a copy of partition 2's data.

Figure 5-2c shows what happens when node N5 comes back up. That partition of the data is again mapped to node N5 and the other two map columns slide back to the right. They go back to being in the succession list for that partition.

Given the fixed number of partitions, 4,096, and the IDs of the nodes, the partition map is computable. Every node in the cluster knows the ID of every other node in the cluster when time nodes are added or removed from the cluster. Hence, each node in the cluster can compute the partition map and thus knows where every data partition resides without having to communicate with each other.

There is more complexity to this. In larger clusters where there are fewer partitions per node, it is necessary to sacrifice some data migration minimization to get a more even data load spread. Rack awareness introduces another complicating factor as well. Feel free to dive into the docs or academic papers published by Aerospike to get more details if you wish.

Cluster Self-Management

The Aerospike cluster management subsystem self-manages all of this partitioning, mapping, and migration. It ensures that all the nodes have a consensus on the cluster's current membership.

Events such as network faults and node arrival or departure trigger cluster membership changes. These changes can be both planned and unplanned. Examples include randomly occurring network disruptions, scheduled capacity increments, and hardware/software upgrades.

The three components to clustering are:

The heartbeat subsystem
> Maintains the adjacency list (described later in the chapter) and stores the latest heartbeat exchanged to keep track of when nodes are added or removed

The clustering subsystem
    Maintains the succession list

The exchange subsystem
    Exchanges partition data and invokes partition balance

The specific objectives of the cluster management subsystem are:

- Arrive at a single consistent view of current cluster members across all nodes in the cluster.
- Automatically detect new node arrival/departure and seamlessly reconfigure the cluster.
- Detect network faults and be resilient to such network flakiness.
- Minimize time to detect and adapt to cluster membership changes.

Cluster View

Each Aerospike node is automatically assigned a unique node identifier, which is a function of its node ID or MAC address and the listening port. Cluster view is defined by the tuple `<cluster_key, succession_list>`, where:

- `cluster_key` is a randomly generated 8-byte value that identifies an instance of the cluster view.
- `succession_list` is an ordered list of unique cluster node identifiers.

The cluster key uniquely identifies the current cluster membership state and changes every time the cluster view changes. It enables Aerospike nodes to differentiate between two cluster views with an identical set of member nodes.

Every change to the cluster view significantly affects operation latency and the performance of the entire system. This means there is a need to quickly detect node arrival/departure events for an efficient consensus mechanism to handle any changes to the cluster view.

However, migrating data when a node is not down (it may just have a flaky network connection for instance) would be very inefficient. So, it is important not to act until a node is down for certain.

Node arrival or departure is detected via heartbeat messages exchanged periodically between nodes. Every node in the cluster maintains an adjacency list, which is the list of other nodes that have recently sent heartbeat messages to this node. Nodes departing the cluster are detected by the absence of heartbeat messages for a configurable timeout interval; after this, they are removed from the adjacency list.

The main objectives of the detection mechanism are:

- To avoid declaring nodes as departed because of sporadic and momentary network glitches.
- To prevent an erratic node from frequently joining and departing from the cluster. A node could behave erratically due to system-level resource bottlenecks in the use of CPU, network, storage device, etc.

Alternatives such as replica writes can also be used as a secondary surrogate for heartbeat messages. The cluster view is unchanged as long as a primary or secondary heartbeat message is received within the timeout interval.

Potential node failure is anticipated automatically. Every node in the cluster evaluates the health score of each of its neighboring nodes by computing the average message loss from that node.

An erratically behaving node typically has a high average message loss. If an unhealthy node is a member of the cluster, it is removed from the cluster. If it is not yet a member, it is not considered for membership until its average message loss falls within tolerable limits.

Cluster View Changes

Changes to the adjacency list trigger a run of the Aerospike clustering algorithm that arrives at the new cluster view. Aerospike works to minimize the number of transitions the cluster would undergo as an effect of a single fault event.

For example, a faulty network switch could make a subset of the cluster members unreachable. Once the network is restored, there would be a need to add all these nodes back to the cluster. To minimize cluster transitions, which are fairly expensive in terms of time and resources, nodes make cluster change decisions only at the start of fixed, configurable cluster change intervals.

The idea is to avoid reacting too quickly to node arrival and departure events, as detected by the heartbeat subsystem, and instead process a batch of adjacent node events with a single cluster view change. Aerospike's cluster management scheme allows for multiple node additions or removals at a time without downtime.

Intelligent Clients

Databases don't exist in isolation. The full stack needs to function so that the end-to-end system scales. An intelligent client layer absorbs the complexity of managing the cluster. There are various challenges to overcome here and a few of them are addressed here:

Discovery

Clients use one or more seed nodes, which tells them about every adjacent node until the client knows the role and existence of every node in the cluster. The partition map (see Figure 5-2), showing the relationship of partitions to nodes, is exchanged and cached within the clients. With that partition map, clients are always a single hop from the data. The partition map identifies the data's exact location, eliminating the need for any intermediate routing nodes.

Information sharing

Each client process stores the partition map in memory. To keep the information up to date, the client process periodically consults the server nodes to check for any updates. It does this by checking the version it has stored locally against the latest version of the server. If there is an update, it requests the full partition map.

Cluster Node Handling

For each cluster node, at the time of initialization, the client creates an in-memory structure on behalf of that node and stores its partition map. It also maintains a connection pool for that node.

When a node is considered down, the partition map, in-memory structure, and connection pool are all torn down. The setup and teardown is a costly operation. If the underlying network is flaky and this repeatedly happens, it can degrade the performance of the overall system. This means a sophisticated approach to identifying cluster node health is needed. Aerospike has a couple of systems to help:

Health score

A transient network issue or other problem may make it seem like a node is down while the server node is actually up and healthy. Clients track the number of failures encountered on database operations at a specific node. The client drops a cluster node only when the failure count (aka "happiness factor") crosses a particular threshold. Any successful operation to that node will reset the failure count to 0. This scheme is implemented by default in the client libraries.

Cluster consultation

Flaky networks are often tough to handle. One-way network failures (A sees B, but B does not see A) are even tougher. There can be situations where the cluster nodes can see each other but the client is unable to see some cluster nodes directly (say, X). In these cases, the client consults all the known nodes of the cluster to see if any of them have X in their neighbor list. If a node reports that X is in its neighbor list, the client does nothing. If X is not in any client-visible node's neighbor list, the client will wait for a threshold time, and then remove the node by tearing down the data structures that reference it.

Through the years, these automatic schemes have proven to greatly improve system stability.

Scale Up

Scaling out to multiple nodes is something that all distributed systems have in common. Aerospike technology is also focused on scaling up to take advantage of every bit of network, storage, and processing capacity available within each node.

In this section, you'll learn about the Hybrid Memory Architecture (HMA) that enables tens of terabytes of data in flash storage to be read and written per node with submillisecond latency. You'll also learn about system-level techniques that leverage multicore processors to help Aerospike scale up to millions of transactions per second per node at submillisecond latencies.

Aerospike's ability to scale up on nodes effectively and use flash storage means the following:

- Scaling up to higher throughput levels on fewer nodes.
- Better availability, since the probability of a node failure typically increases as the number of nodes in a cluster increases.
- Lower total cost of ownership as storing and accessing data in real time from flash storage devices is less expensive than storing and accessing it from memory.
- Easier operational footprint. Managing a 20-node cluster versus a 200-node cluster is a huge win for operators.

Hybrid Memory Architecture

Most databases store both data and indexes together on disk. In-memory databases store both data and indexes together in memory. To take full advantage of each compute node, Aerospike heavily leverages SSDs (flash storage devices) to store data. The database has implemented bespoke algorithms so that it can access data on SSD with submillisecond latency. Indexes, however, are stored separately in memory (RAM or PMEM). This is the heart of the patented Hybrid Memory Architecture™ (HMA) (Figure 5-3).

Aerospike data access is implemented using a proprietary filesystem layer, so it bypasses the operating system's filesystem layer. Unlike most databases, Aerospike also does not utilize a page cache when reading, which removes another layer as shown in Figure 5-3. The index, which is fully resident in memory, points to the actual data item on the flash drive location, allowing reads within a millisecond.

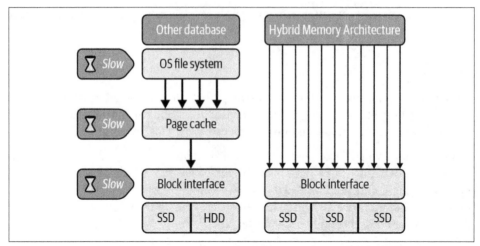

Figure 5-3. Hybrid Memory Architecture compared to standard filesystem-based database architecture

Writes can't be done directly on the SSD due to wear leveling issues where you can burn out portions of the SSD if you overwrite them too often. Aerospike implemented a log structure filesystem with large block writers, plus copy-on-write semantics so that SSD writes are gathered in memory in buffers and then flushed to flash storage. This allows Aerospike to manage very heavy read loads at high performance, even when in the presence of very heavy write loads.

Here is a summary of SSD strategies:

Direct SSD device access
    Not filtered through an operating system's filesystem layer

Highly parallelized
    Designed to take full advantage of multi-SSD nodes

Large block writes to SSD
    Reduces wear on SSD cells to extend life of hardware

SSD optimized
    Gets the best possible read and write performance

Continuous, nondisruptive defragmentation
    Prevents running out of space on disk

The end result of all this is an increase in the amount of data you can store in a node, in proportion to the amount of SSDs on the node, not just the amount of memory. This means that the number of nodes in a large Aerospike cluster is typically an order of magnitude less than comparable systems that store all the data in memory.

For example, Aerospike would use 20 nodes to do the same work as an in-memory transactional database on 200 nodes.

Multicore Processors

For this to work in practice, Aerospike also has to run 10× the transactions on each node. This requires taking advantage of multicore processors and multi-CPU nodes.

Aerospike uses multiple strategies to make this work, including:

- Multithreading
- Highly efficient C code
- CPU-pinning (such as NUMA-pinning done in collaboration with Intel)
- Thread binding to specific network queues (ADQ [Application Device Queue] binding to CPU threads, for example, optimized for particular Intel hardware cards)
- Using parallel network queues to avoid bottlenecks on particular CPUs
- Running in the network listener thread to avoid costs associated with thread context switches

All of these together allow Aerospike to drive millions of transactions per second through a single node.

As benchmarks such as the one in Figure 5-4 have shown, these strategies can run as many as 8 million transactions per second, or with network hardware optimizations such as Intel's ADQ, 15 million transactions per second through a single node. In practice, you are unlikely to need that many transactions on a single node, but it is useful to know that the headroom exists.

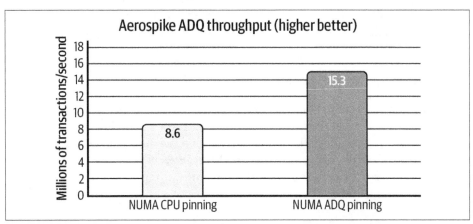

Figure 5-4. Benchmark example showing large headroom for transactions

Taking full advantage of CPU capabilities is one strategy that helps Aerospike run very high-throughput, low-latency workloads at very high scale on small cluster sizes.

Memory Fragmentation

Aerospike handles all its memory allocation natively rather than depending on the programming language or on a runtime system. Aerospike keeps the index packed into RAM. With sizes at high scale over 100 GB and high transaction rates, memory fragmentation is a major challenge. Using a specific memory allocator library (*jemalloc* (*https://oreil.ly/nfkyi*)) and other strategies like grouping objects by namespace, Aerospike optimizes the long-term object creation, access, modification, and deletion pattern and minimizes fragmentation.

Data Structure Design

For data structures like indexes and global structures that need concurrent access, Aerospike keeps all critical data structures in single-threaded partitions, each with a separate lock. This reduces contention across partitions. Access to nested data structures like index trees does not involve acquiring multiple locks at each level. Instead, each tree element has both a reference count and its own lock. This allows for safe and concurrent read, write, and delete access to the index, without holding multiple locks.

These structures are carefully designed to make sure that frequently and commonly accessed data has locality and falls within a single cache line in order to reduce cache misses (when the application requests data from a cache, but it isn't there) and data stalls (time spent waiting for data to be retrieved). For example, the index entry in Aerospike is exactly 64 bytes, the same size as a cache line.

In production systems like Aerospike, the functional aspects, system monitoring, and troubleshooting features need to be built in and optimized. This information is maintained in a thread-local data structure and can be pulled and aggregated together at query time.

Scheduling and Prioritization

In addition to basic key-value store (KVS) operations, Aerospike supports batch queries, scans, and secondary index queries. Scans are generally slow background jobs that walk through the entire data set. Batch and secondary index queries return a matched subset of the data and, therefore, have different levels of selectivity based on the particular use case. Balancing throughput and fairness with such a varied workload is a challenge.

This is achieved by following three major principles:

Partition jobs based on their type
> Each job type is allocated its own thread pool and is prioritized across pools. Jobs of a specific type are further prioritized within their own pool.

Effort-based unit of work
> The basic unit of work is the effort needed to process a single record including lookup, I/O, and validation. Each job is composed of multiple units of work, which defines its effort.

Controlled load generation
> The thread pool has a load generator, which controls the rate of generation of work. It is the threads in the pool that perform the work.

Aerospike uses cooperative scheduling whereby worker threads yield CPU for other workers to finish their job after X units of work. These workers have CPU core and partition affinity to avoid data contention when parallel workers are accessing certain data.

Concurrent workloads of a certain basic job type in Aerospike are generally run on a first-come, first-served basis to allow for low latency for each request. The system also needs the ability to make progress in longer-running workloads like scans and queries, which are sometimes guided by user settings and/or by the application's ability to consume the result set. For such cases, the system, as illustrated in Figure 5-5, dynamically adapts and shifts to round-robin scheduling of tasks. This means many tasks that are run in parallel are paused and rescheduled dynamically, based on the progress they can make.

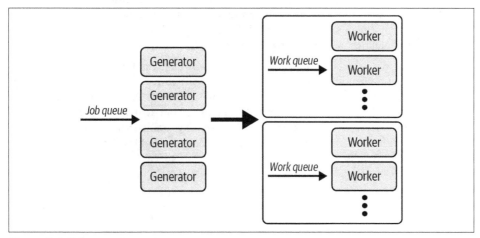

Figure 5-5. Job management

Parallelism

Aerospike's uniform data partitioning enables parallel processing using system resources in a balanced and efficient manner. Many Aerospike nodes are configured with multiple SSD storage devices. In addition to uniformly distributing data across nodes, Aerospike data can also be distributed randomly into these storage devices, providing extremely high levels of parallelism on small clusters.

This provides the opportunity for even higher levels of parallelism on low numbers of nodes. Figure 5-6 shows a system that contains four nodes with five SSDs each, a small example system.

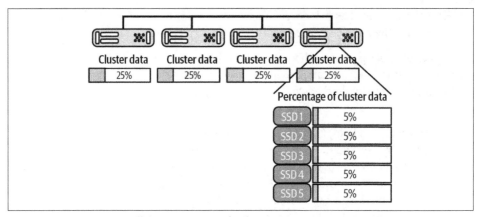

Figure 5-6. 20-Way parallelism on a 4-node cluster

This simple example illustrates that a 100-node cluster with 16 storage devices per node can drive a 1600-way parallel execution of a high-throughput workload of individual record writes in the millions of transactions per second.

With the scale up available in an HMA configuration using multithreading on multicore processor architectures with parallel network queues, up to a theoretical limit of 256 TiB can be stored per node. Most practical implementations top out at 100 TB per node, resulting in database storage of 10 petabytes on that same 100-node cluster that can be processed at a very high rate of throughput with submillisecond read/write latency.

Distributed Transaction Consistency

Aerospike uses all the performance its scale out and scale up capabilities provide to make transactional algorithms with strong consistency. Note that, at the time of writing, Aerospike supports strong consistency for single-record transactions with replication (multirecord transaction support is expected in a future release). This high performance level enables Aerospike algorithms to use strategies that aren't available to other systems that are slower on the same underlying infrastructure.

This section covers the basics of how transactional consistency is guaranteed in an Aerospike cluster, and how transactions can be implemented when components are separated geographically.

Strong Consistency in Transactions

The CAP theorem of distributed databases essentially states that while there are three important aspects to distributed databases, namely consistency, availability, and partition tolerance, one aspect must always be sacrificed to keep the other two high. Which two are chosen determines how the database functions. Partition tolerance is necessary for distributing data and workload across a cluster, so the choices are generally AP, which emphasizes availability, or CP, which emphasizes data consistency.

Aerospike can be configured in AP mode, which prioritizes availability over consistency. It is uncommon to violate consistency in a properly running Aerospike system even in AP mode, except during the following two scenarios:

1. When the cluster splits into two or more subclusters that continue to take reads and writes.
2. When a cluster simultaneously loses a number of nodes or racks that is equal to or greater than the replication factor and continues to take reads and writes.

Roster

One key difference between Aerospike and other distributed databases is that Aerospike does not use quorums in the way other databases do. The only quorum is a simple write all and read one copy, which is possible due to Aerospike's level of write and read performance. Instead of quorum, Aerospike uses a roster-based strong consistency scheme.

When configured for strong consistency, Aerospike defines a roster as the set of nodes that are intended to be present. When all the roster nodes are present, and all the partitions are in their correct computed location, the cluster is in its steady state and provides optimal performance.

As we described earlier, partitions are assigned to nodes in a cluster using a random assignment. For data redundancy, each partition will be copied the number of times determined by the replication factor, a configurable setting.

One of these partition copies is referred to as roster-master and the rest roster-replica:

roster-master
> The roster-master refers to the node that would house the primary copy of a specific data partition.

roster-replica
> The roster-replica refers to the node or nodes that would house secondary copies of a specific data partition.

 The roster and partition map is on ALL nodes, even if they are disconnected from the rest of the cluster. This means that every node knows where every partition is, even if communication between nodes is cut off.

Along with the cluster roster is the concept of a majority and supermajority of the roster:

Majority
> More than half the total number of nodes in the roster.

Supermajority
> More than the total number of nodes in the roster minus the replication setting.

For example, in a cluster with 10 nodes and a replication factor of 3, a majority would be 6 or more nodes. A supermajority would be 8, 9, or 10 nodes, more than 10 – 3. The majority and supermajority are important for determining full availability in split-brain conditions.

Split-Brain Conditions

When network connectivity drops between nodes in a cluster, this essentially creates two functional subclusters that can continue to function to some extent. This is called a split-brain condition. As discussed in Chapter 1, most systems for providing strong consistency require a minimum of three copies (*https://oreil.ly/T-sRg*). So, if a cluster splits, one of the two subclusters can allow writes if it has a majority (two out of three) of copies of the data item. Aerospike optimizes this further by regularly storing only two copies but using an adaptive scheme that adds more write copies on the fly in situations where they are necessary, thus optimizing the performance in most cases.

Note that even a two-copy system still needs a minimum of three nodes to preserve availability. A single node will never have both the master and replica of the same partition. The Aerospike replication scheme provides an equivalent level of availability with two copies as a traditional quorum-based system using three copies. This reduction continues to grow as the replication factor increases—where other systems store N replicas, Aerospike only needs to store $(N / 2) + 1$ to achieve a similar availability level during common network failures. As an example, to allow two nodes to be out of the cluster at any time, Aerospike needs three data copies. Quorum-based systems need five copies.

A partition is available and active for both reads and writes in CP mode if:

1. A subcluster has *both* the roster-master and all the roster-replicas for a partition.

2. A subcluster contains *a majority* of nodes in the full roster and has *either* the roster-master or a roster-replica.

3. A subcluster has *exactly half* of the nodes in the full roster, and it has the *roster-master* for a partition.

4. A subcluster has a supermajority of the nodes in the full roster.

Some nodes are excluded while counting the majority and super-majority conditions:

- A previously departed node that rejoins the cluster with missing data (e.g., one or more empty storage devices)
- A node that was not cleanly shut down that has been enabled

These nodes will have an *evade* flag set until they are properly inducted into the cluster with all data.

Let's look at some examples to make this clearer. For simplicity, assume the replication factor is set to 2 in these examples. Every partition in the system will have one roster-master and one roster-replica.

Start with a small 5-node cluster, with the roster-master of a particular partition's data on node 5 and the roster-replica on node 4 (illustrated in Figure 5-7a). In this situation, the roster is whole and the data partition is fully active for both reads and writes.

If network communication with nodes 4 and 5 is lost, they are cut off from the rest of the cluster, creating essentially two subclusters as in Figure 5-7b. Since both the roster-master and roster-replica for a partition are in one subcluster and no copy of that data exists in the other subcluster, only the smaller cluster remains available for that partition for both reads and writes.

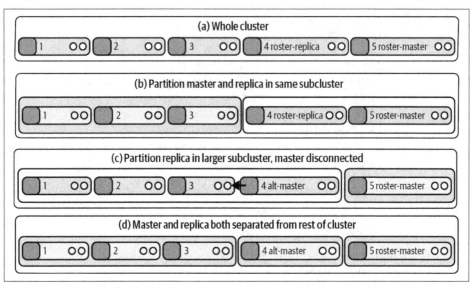

Figure 5-7. Roster and split-brain situations

Now, suppose that only node 5 is disconnected or down, possibly due to a rolling upgrade. This isolates the roster-master from the rest of the cluster, but the replica of that partition remains. Because the roster-master is in a smaller minority cluster, but a replica is in the majority cluster, the rule is that this partition of data becomes unavailable in the smaller cluster, which is just node 5 in the example in Figure 5-7c.

Temporarily, the roster-replica will be promoted to master (alt-master) and a second replica (alt-replica) created on another node according to the succession list in the partition map. In the example in Figure 5-7c, the data is replicated on node 3. Because every node has the roster and partition map, the new data location can still be computed by all nodes. This allows writes to maintain consistency and durability, and the partition remains live for both reads and writes. In any two-cluster split-brain situation, data partitions will be 100% available in either one subcluster or the other, never in both.

If this was a case of a *rolling upgrade*, node 5 would become active again after being upgraded and would rejoin the cluster. Node 4 would be taken down next. Between node 5, which has all data from before it went down, and node 3, which has all changes made to the data while node 5 was down, a complete picture of the data is still available for any request. A read might be slightly slower due to having to check both nodes to make sure the latest changes are included, but in general, there would be no disruption of reads or writes, 100% availability. For more information on rolling upgrades, check the Aerospike documentation (*https://oreil.ly/azlUV*).

In Figure 5-7d is an example of a possible split-brain condition where the partition would be completely unavailable. In this situation, the master is isolated as is the replica, each in a separate subcluster. This is an example of the CAP theorem in action. In order to maintain strong consistency, availability would be sacrificed in this instance.

Writes

Writes in Aerospike are always a *write all* mechanism, meaning that if a write is done on a database with a replication factor of 2, it will always write 2 copies of the data changes. If the replication factor is 3, it will always write 3 copies.

Figure 5-8 shows a write in a 3-copy system (replication factor set to 3):

1. The client initiates a write to the master node for that partition's data.
2. The master node writes the data locally.
3. The master node copies the data changes to the two replicas in parallel.
4. The replica nodes write the data locally and then respond back to the master that the data copies were successful.
5. The master commits the transaction and communicates the commit to all replicas. This "Advise Replicated" message does not wait for a response from the replicas and so is very quick.
6. The master communicates the successful write back to the client.

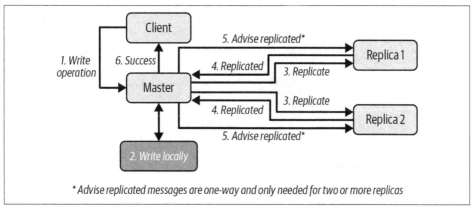

Figure 5-8. Synchronous write logic

The CAP theorem tends to be thought of as having two types of consistency, either strong consistency or eventual consistency, but there is a type of slightly lower form of strong consistency: sequential consistency, also known as session consistency. For reads, Aerospike supports linearizability and sequential consistency. In the case of writes, though, they are always strongly consistent. There is no data loss tolerated.

Rack Awareness

Rack awareness, an Aerospike Enterprise Edition feature, means that a distributed application is aware of which nodes are on which racks in a datacenter (or cloud regions and availability zones). Since Aerospike is rack aware, it will not store both the master and replicas of a partition on the same rack. This is so that if the entire rack is lost, the database can continue functioning normally on another rack.

Rack awareness has a very strong advantage as far as performance for reads. If the data is available on multiple racks, you can access the data on a single rack for reads as if it were local. Writes, though, must always access multiple partition copies, and multiple racks in the case of a rack-aware cluster.

However, since a complete copy of the data is known to be available, in some situations, Aerospike can continue to function for both reads and writes with both availability and consistency when communication between racks is down. An example of when that capability is essential is when racks are geographically separated (Figure 5-9).

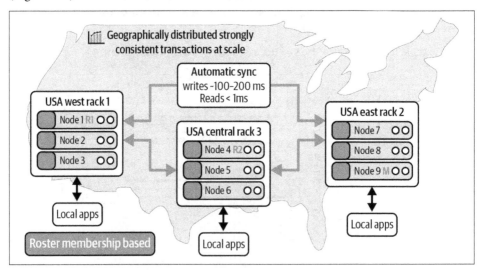

Figure 5-9. Geographically distributed database

In certain types of use cases, such as interbank money transfers, it is necessary for a single database to span multiple geographically separated locations. In this case, the trade-off is a much higher write latency, but the data remains consistent and reliable, which is more important in this sort of use case.

The example in Figure 5-9 is a three-replica system with three racks spread across the continental United States. Each site has a full copy of the data. The rack awareness allows local client applications to read data locally at extremely low latency, under 1 millisecond. The writes will take considerably longer since they must write to all three racks and are subject to network delays, speed of light limitations, etc. These generally fall between 100 and 300 millisecond delays.

The result of this configuration is a completely *synchronous active/active system*. If an entire rack goes down, or connectivity to it is lost, causing a split-brain situation, the other two racks can continue to run with both availability and strong consistency without causing any conflicts.

When a rack goes out or rejoins, no operator intervention is required to keep the database running smoothly. It's taken care of automatically. For you, this means very high uptime, with the only trade-off being higher write latency.

Depending on how you configure the geodistributed database, instead of trading write latency, you can choose to lose some data consistency in an *asynchronous active-active system*. Cross-datacenter replication (XDR), also an Aerospike Enterprise Edition feature, transparently and asynchronously replicates data between Aerospike clusters. Companies often use XDR to replicate data from Aerospike-based edge systems to a centralized Aerospike system. XDR also enables companies to support continuous operations during a crisis (such as a natural disaster) that takes down an entire cluster.

Read the Aerospike documentation for more information on the various options.

Summary

Aerospike architecture is far more involved than would make sense to discuss in a basic up-and-running book. Rather than drown you in details, this should provide you with the foundational knowledge to build on. This essential understanding will help you get the most out of the database right from the start.

Next, we'll dive into modeling data in Aerospike.

## CHAPTER 6

Data Modeling

In the previous chapters, you looked at the Aerospike architecture and the facilities the database provides. In this chapter we will discuss how to model data in Aerospike to solve common problems. As with most databases, there are a variety of techniques that can be used to solve the same problem, so we will address some of the pros and cons of various approaches.

Note that there are many different ways to model data in Aerospike, and the appropriate technique depends on the problem trying to be solved. This chapter will introduce some of the more common techniques, but it is by no means exhaustive.

Aerospike Data Modeling

Aerospike supports records that have a structure similar to a relational database and it supports secondary indexes similar to a relational database, so it would seem intuitive that data modeling techniques would be similar to those used in relational databases. However, this is not always the case. To illustrate this, let's look at a classical way of aggregating data.

Suppose you want to model a customer record. The customer has zero or more addresses associated with it, and the addresses have no business use if they are not associated with a customer. This is the classical case of aggregation and you can represent this as shown in Figure 6-1.

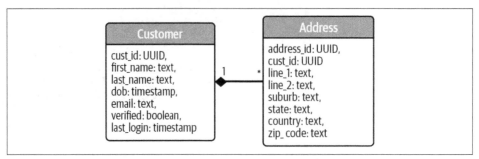

Figure 6-1. Entity–relationship model of a customer with their addresses

In a relational model, you would create two distinct tables, customer and address, with a foreign key from the address to the customer. To preserve referential integrity, you would cascade any deletes from the customer table to the address table. This might be defined in PostgreSQL syntax similar to:

```
CREATE TABLE customer( cust_id UUID PRIMARY KEY, first_name TEXT, ...
    last_login TIMESTAMP);
CREATE TABLE address ( address_id UUID PRIMARY KEY,
    line_1 TEXT NOT NULL, line_2 TEXT, ...
    cust_id UUID REFERENCES customer(cust_id) ON DELETE CASCADE);
```

In order to get good performance when you want to load all the addresses for a customer, you should put an index on the foreign key of the address:

```
CREATE INDEX CUST_ID_IDX on ADDRESS(CUST_ID);
```

Consider the same problem in Aerospike. You want to be able to load the addresses for a customer efficiently, and if the customer goes away you need the associated addresses to be removed too. There are a couple of ways of modeling this. Let's take a look at the pros and cons of each.

A quick reminder of some differences and equivalencies between Aerospike and most relational databases.

Relational DBs	Aerospike
Database	Namespace
Table	Set
Record	Record
Field	Bin

Secondary Indexes

This problem could be modeled in Aerospike very similarly to the classical technique. You could have two sets, a Customer set and an Address set. The Address set could have a bin that contains the Customer ID and a secondary index defined on the bin, as shown in Figure 6-2.

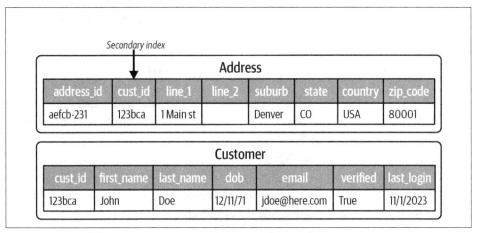

Figure 6-2. Modeling an aggregation with a secondary index

There are a couple of problems with this approach:

1. Aerospike does not support automatic cascade on deletion. When you remove the Customer object, the associated Address objects should be removed too. This cannot be achieved automatically with this data model. It should be fairly easy to do this with a secondary index coupled with an operation, but this would include the overhead of multiple operations, an explicit deletion of the Customer object, then the secondary index scan over the Address objects. Example code would be:

```
String custToDelete = "123bca";
Statement stmt = new Statement();
stmt.setNamespace("test");
stmt.setSetName("address");
stmt.setFilter(Filter.equal("cust_id", custToDelete));
ExecuteTask task = client.execute(null, stmt, Operation.delete());
client.delete(null, new Key("test", "customer", custToDelete));
task.waitTillComplete();
```

2. This is not a very efficient use of a secondary index. Remember that, as mentioned in Chapter 4, secondary index queries are performed via a "scatter gather" approach where all nodes are queried for matching records in parallel, then the results are streamed back to the client. This results in a decent amount of work for both the Aerospike client driver and the cluster. If there are only a handful of addresses and a large number of nodes in the cluster, many of the nodes will do work checking to see if they have any matching addresses without finding any.

Let's take a look at a more efficient approach: aggregating the addresses into the customer.

Aggregating Subobjects into One Record

In this use case there are typically only a handful of addresses associated with a single customer, and the addresses are typically small. Why not just store the addresses inside the customer record itself?

Using this approach you would define an address bin on the customer record. This bin would contain a list and the list elements would be maps. Each map would hold one address, with the map keys being the fields of the map (city, state, country, etc.) and the values being the associated data. For example:

```
{
    "cust_id": "123bca",
    "first_name": "John",
    "last_name": "Doe",
    "dob": 1680714616850,
    "email": "jdoe@here.com",
    "verified": true,
    "last_login": 1685764613895
    "addresses": [
        {
            "line_1": "1 Main St",
            "city": "Denver",
            "state": "CO",
            "country": "USA",
            "Zip_code": 80001
        }]
}
```

This approach offers several advantages:

- Reading a customer record automatically retrieves all the addresses for that customer without needing to perform an additional query. Conversely, removing a Customer record automatically removes all the addresses too.

- The customer and the addresses are accessed using key-value operations, which are incredibly efficient in Aerospike.

- Addresses can still be directly manipulated or added/removed from the customer using list and map operations.

- The Address object is simplified. There's no longer any need for the Address to contain the Customer ID—you must already know the Customer ID to access the addresses. Also, there is no need for an Address ID on each Address—the place in the list could potentially serve as a "pseudo-ID" if needed.

If you're thinking that this will increase the size of the customer record, you are correct. But the number of addresses would normally be fairly small, meaning the overhead of this approach is typically low. In fact, the penalty for the larger objects might be smaller than you think. Remember that Aerospike typically uses SSDs to store information and most modern SSDs are "block-level" devices, meaning that data can only be read or written in blocks, rather than individual bytes. This block size is typically 4 KiB, so if your application asks an SSD for 1 KiB, the SSD will typically read 4 KiB and throw away 3 KiB. If adding the addresses increases the size of the customer record from say 2 KiB to 3 KiB, the cost of reading the record from storage will be exactly the same!

Aggregating Subobjects into Multiple Records

The preceding approach works well if the number of subobjects is known to be finitely bound to a small number. However, there are many use cases where this is not the case. Consider a credit card with the associated transactions. The number of transactions might add up to thousands per year for heavy credit card users, or significantly higher if the credit card is a corporate card.

One approach for this scenario would be to use a secondary index as discussed in "Secondary Indexes" on page 99, with each transaction storing the account number. To query the transactions for a given account, a secondary index lookup could be performed. However, credit card providers typically need just the transactions for a recent date range, like the last 180 days. Secondary indexes using the account number could be combined with an expression as shown in Chapter 4 to solve this problem. However, if the credit card was a corporate credit card, for example, with millions of transactions, the database cluster will need to load all of these transactions, filter out the desired ones using expressions, and sort the results, all of which may take longer than the fraud detection window.

To speed this up, consider an approach where the Transaction records are merged into the CreditCard record. A record for this CreditCard might look similar to the following, with the primary account number (PAN), typically a part of the credit card number, used as the PK:

```
{
    "cardNo": "1234123412341234",
    "cardSeqNo": 1,
    "custNo": "cust-1234",
    "expiry": 1680714616850,
    "opened": 1678912262162,
    "txns": [
        {
            "txnId": "txn1",
            "amount": 10000,
            "desc": "New car tire",
            "txnDate": 1680113831954
        },
        {
            "txnId": "txn2",
            "amount": 500,
            "desc": "Ice cream",
            "txnDate": 1699422631954
        }
    ]
}
```

In this case, it is not possible to store all of these transactions in a single record. As of Aerospike version 6.4, the largest record that can be stored is limited to 8 MiB. Even if you could store everything in 8 MiB, would you really want to? As discussed in Chapter 5, Aerospike always performs *copy on write*, meaning that every time a record changes, the entire record will be rewritten. So making one trivial change—such as adding a single transaction—on an 8 MiB CreditCard record means that the storage device will read 8 MiB and then 8 MiB will be written back to the storage device with the change. This is a heavy load on the storage device, and if operations such as this are common, the database nodes will likely run out of I/O capacity, slowing the database down. This is illustrated in Figure 6-3.

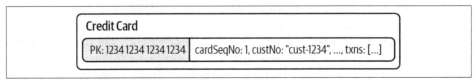

Figure 6-3. Modeling transactions inside a CreditCard record

A better solution to this problem is to separate the large number of child objects into finite "buckets" and store each bucket in a single record. For the credit card example, you could store the transactions in a Transaction set, and store all the transactions for a credit card separated into multiple records, one record per day. So, instead of the data being stored like in Figure 6-3, the new sets might look like in Figure 6-4.

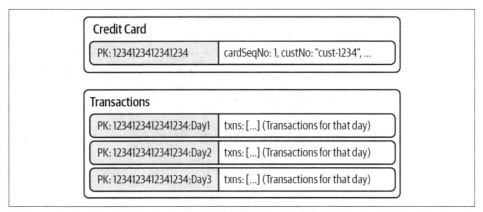

Figure 6-4. Modeling transactions outside of the CreditCard object in daily buckets

In this new model, the CreditCard details become their own record. These typically don't change very often, so rewriting them whenever a transaction is added would be inefficient, but this would happen in the data model depicted in Figure 6-3. Transactions have been separated into a single record per day and these records have compound keys (a key comprised of 2 or more discrete pieces of information) containing both the credit card PAN and a day index from some offset.

Note that the offset day is not important so long as it's consistently used. For example, it might be set to 1/1/2010 as Day 0. The day offset can then easily be calculated as:

```
(milliseconds(NOW) - milliseconds(OFFSET_DATE)) /
TimeUnit.DAYS.toMillis(1);
```

Within the record for a particular day, there is a `txns` bin that stores the transactions for that day. There are various formats that could be used to store these, such as a list of maps shown earlier in this section. In this case, you could change it up a bit and use a map of maps with the timestamp of the transaction as the map key, and the rest of the transaction contained as a map in the value. An example of this might be:

```
txns: {
1680113831954: {"amount": 10000, "desc": "New car tire", "txnId": "txn1"}
1699422631954: {"amount": 500, "desc": "Ice cream", "txnId": "txn2"}
1704423453345: {"amount": 2750, "desc": "Pizza", "txnId": "txn3"}
    ...
}
```

The reason for this change is that use cases on credit card transactions often call for operations based on time ranges, such as "retrieve all transactions between 3 p.m. and 5 p.m. on this date." Having the timestamp as the transaction key makes these operations easier. Similarly, the map would likely be defined as KEY_ORDERED, so time-range-based operations are more efficient. We will describe this in more depth later in "Additional Operations on This Model" on page 106.

Thus, you could write a method to load the last 30 days of transactions for a credit card to run fraud detection checks as:

```
private final static long EPOCH_TIME
        = new GregorianCalendar(2010, 0, 1).getTime().getTime();

private long calculateDaysSinceEpoch(Date date) {
    return (date.getTime()- EPOCH_TIME) / TimeUnit.DAYS.toMillis(1);
}

public List<Transaction> readCreditCardTransactions(IAerospikeClient client,
long cardId) {
    long dayOffset = calculateDaysSinceEpoch(new Date());
    Key[] keys = new Key[DAYS_TO_FETCH];
    for (int i = 0; i < DAYS_TO_FETCH; i++) {
        keys[i] = new Key(creditCardNamespace, SET_NAME,
                        "Pan-" + cardId + ":" + (dayOffset - i));
    }
    Record records[] = client.get(null, keys);
    List<Transaction> txnList = new ArrayList<>();
    for (int i = 0; i < DAYS_TO_FETCH; i++) {
        if (records[i] == null) {
            continue;
        }
        TreeMap<Long, Map<String, Object>> map =
                    (TreeMap<Long,Map<String,Object>>)records[i].getMap(MAP_BIN);
        for (long txnDate : map.descendingKeySet()) {
            Map<String, Object> data = map.get(txnDate);
            Transaction txn = new Transaction();
            txn.setTxnId((String)data.get("txnId"));
            txn.setTxnDate(new Date(txnDate));
            txn.setAmount((long)data.get("amount"));
            txn.setDescription((String)data.get("desc"));
            txnList.add(txn);
        }
    }
    return txnList;
}
```

Let's take a look at what this method is doing.

First, `EPOCH_TIME` is defined to be the number of milliseconds since 1/1/2010. Then a method `calculateDaysSinceEpoch` calculates the number of days since the epoch. This uses 64-bit integer arithmetic, so it's very efficient.

In the method `readCreditCardTransactions`, the first line calls the `calculateDaysSinceEpoch` method to calculate the offset of the current day. This will be a number, something like 5,128, depending on the current date. Then an array of keys is formed with one key for each day in the desired range:

```
Key[] keys = new Key[DAYS_TO_FETCH];
for (int i = 0; i < DAYS_TO_FETCH; i++) {
    keys[i] = new Key(creditCardNamespace, SET_NAME,
                      "Pan-" + cardId + ":" + (dayOffset - i));
}
```

Note that due to its use of constant hashing for record distribution, Aerospike does not have any built-in support for compound keys like some other databases. However, as this example shows, it is possible to build your own. In this case, you use a combination of a fixed string, the `cardId`, and the `dayOffset`. An example of a key generated by this section of code might be `Pan1234123412341234:5125`.

Once the array of keys has been formed, you can call:

```
Record records[] = client.get(null, keys);
```

This call loads all the records passed in the keys array from the database and returns an array of records, one per key as discussed in Chapter 3. This call is typically very efficient, using parallelization across the cluster to get all the results very quickly.

Next, the program iterates through the returned records:

```
List<Transaction> txnList = new ArrayList<>();
for (int i = 0; i < DAYS_TO_FETCH; i++) {
    if (records[i] == null) {
        continue;
    }
```

It is possible that some of the returned records are `null`, which will happen when no transactions were performed on a particular day. In this case, there is no processing to be done, so the day is just skipped.

Next, the method extracts the transaction data from the record:

```
TreeMap<Long, Map<String, Object>> map =
        (TreeMap<Long,Map<String,Object>>)records[i].getMap(MAP_BIN);
for (long txnDate : map.descendingKeySet()) {
    Map<String, Object> data = map.get(txnDate);
    Transaction txn = new Transaction();
    txn.setTxnId((String)data.get("txnId"));
```

In this data model, the transactions are stored in a Map on the server. However, the Map on the server is defined as a KEY_ORDERED map, so they are ordered by the transaction timestamp. Maps in Java are inherently unordered, so to preserve this order the Aerospike Java driver returns a TreeMap—an ordered Map. This allows the transactions to be processed in chronological order. This would be very convenient if the use case called for only returning the 1,000 most recent transactions over the previous 30 days, for example.

All that remains is to unpack each transaction into a Transaction object that the application understands. This can be done by pulling each field out of the map and setting it on the Transaction object. This should be fairly familiar if you have unpacked objects using a JDBC driver in Java for a relational database.

Additional Operations on This Model

The map structure allows the records to be queried efficiently by their key, which is conveniently a number representing a date. Aerospike's MapOperation class allows us to perform operations within the map. As a reminder, the data in the map looks like this:

```
txns: {
1680113831954: {"amount": 10000, "desc": "New car tire", "txnId": "txn1"}
1699422631954: {"amount": 500, "desc": "Ice cream", "txnId": "txn2"}
1704423453345: {"amount": 2750, "desc": "Pizza", "txnId": "txn3"}
    ...
}
```

The code in the preceding section gets all the elements of the map and converts them into Transaction objects. But what if you don't want the whole map? For example, you might just want the transactions between 3 p.m. and 5 p.m. on that day. In other words, you might want a range of keys to be returned from the map rather than the full map. This could be achieved using:

```
Record record = client.operate(null, key, MapOperation.getByKeyRange(
        "txns",
        Value.get(startTime),
        Value.get(endTime),
        MapReturnType.KEY_VALUE));
```

In this case, the startTime would be 3 p.m. of the day in question (converted to a long) and endTime would be 5 p.m. on the same day. These long values need to be converted into a Value class in order to be passed to the getByKeyRange method, hence the use of the Value.get(...) methods. The name of the bin holding the map is "txns" and you want both the key and the value to be returned so that the whole transaction can be reassembled.

As discussed in Chapter 4, the `operate` command always returns a `Record`, but the type of the value being returned for the bin being operated on depends on the operation. For example, if you just wanted the count of the transactions between 3 p.m. and 5 p.m., you could have passed `MapReturnType.COUNT` instead of `MapReturn Type.KEY_VALUE`. Then the count could have been retrieved by calling:

```
int count = record.getInt("txns");
```

However, in this case you are getting both the key and the value back, so you can reassemble the transaction. So here Aerospike will return a `List` of `AbstractMap. SimpleEntry`.

This might seem odd. Why would the Aerospike client return a `List` when you selected from a `Map` in the database? Well, remember that Aerospike `Maps` can be sorted (as in this example) and you're selecting a range of keys from that sorted `map`. Java `maps` have no concept of ordering, so the Aerospike client returns the items in the order you requested as an ordered list.

To use this, you could do something like:

```
List<SimpleEntry<Long, Map<String,Object>>> entries =
    (List<SimpleEntry<Long, Map<String, Object>>>)record.getList(MAP_BIN);
for (SimpleEntry<Long, Map<String,Object>> simpleEntry : entries) {
    Long txnTime = simpleEntry.getKey();
    Date txnDate = new Date(txnTime);
    Map<String, Object> txnDetails = simpleEntry.getValue();
    System.out.printf("%tH:%tM:%tS:%s\n",
            txnDate, txnDate, txnDate, txnDetails);
}
```

This will output something similar to:

```
13:49:14:{amount=74, desc=desc-1, txnid=txn-74}
16:18:14:{amount=26, desc=desc-1, txnid=txn-26}
16:35:33:{amount=40, desc=desc-1, txnid=txn-40}
```

Obviously, if you're using real data instead of generated data, the transaction values will be more meaningful.

Further Refinements

The preceding data model is good, but you could potentially make it better. Consider one of the transactions you have stored in the map:

```
1680113831954: {"amount": 10000, "desc": "New car tire", "txnId": "txn1"}
```

Since the transaction date is the map key, you can use `MapOperations` like `getByKey Range`, `getByKeyList`, and so on to perform operations on the data. However, there is a lot of redundancy here as each transaction for a given day contains the same descriptions of the data: `amount`, `desc`, and `txnId`. This will occupy a lot of space in the database—in fact those descriptions will be longer than the actual data being stored!

One way around this is to store the actual data in a list instead of a map. This involves using a data format like the following:

```
txns: {
        1680113831954: [10000, "New car tire", "txn1"],
        1699422631954: [500, "Ice cream", "txn2"],
        1704423453345: [2750, "Pizza", "txn3"],
        ...
}
```

The only difference between inserting the data as a list and inserting it as a map is how the value is constructed:

```
List<Object> transactionAsList = Arrays.asList(
    transaction.getAmount(),
    transaction.getDescription(),
    transaction.getTxnId());

client.operate(null, key,
    MapOperation.put(mapPolicy, MAP_BIN,
    Value.get(transaction.getTxnDate().getTime()),
    Value.get(transactionAsList)));
```

This format now saves substantial space on the storage device, yielding better performance as it needs to read and write less data, send less data across the network, and more transactions can fit within the same record. However, the format is harder to read. While it's not difficult in this simplified example, imagine an object stored in a list that has 20 integer values. If these integers represent different things like dates, transaction amounts, customer IDs, and so on, discerning which integer means what is difficult. If, however, the integers are the same thing, like components of a vector, then a list is the natural structure for them.

There is one other advantage of using a list in this scenario. Lists, unlike maps, have an inherent ordering which can be useful in some use cases.

List ordering

When Aerospike compares two lists to see if they're equal or one is greater than the other, it uses these rules:

1. Compare each element in the list from the first element in the list to the last. If the element being compared is greater than the corresponding element in the other list, this list is greater. If the elements are equal, move onto the next element.

2. Once one list has no more elements, look at the size of the other list. If it is greater than this list, the other list is greater. Otherwise, both lists are equal.

These rules make more sense with examples:

- List [1,2] is less than [1,3] because the first elements in both lists are equal, but 2 < 3.

- Similarly, [1,2,9] is less than [1,3,1] because the second element in the first list is less than the second element in the second list. The fact that the third element in the first list is greater than the third element in the second list is irrelevant.

- List [1,2,3] is greater than list [1,2] because they both contain the same first two elements, but the first list is longer than the second list.

- The other thing to remember with ordering in Aerospike is that types have a predefined order, which you can see here (*https://oreil.ly/0mi2a*), but comparing two items of different types will always result in the same outcome, regardless of the value of that type. To illustrate with an example, integers are always less than strings, which are always less than lists. So 27 is less than "25", which is less than [1], simply by virtue of the types.

Ordering by value

Thus far, you have learned about operations that act on the keys. These operations are typically very efficient especially for maps that are defined as KEY_ORDERED or KEY_VALUE_ORDERED as you learned in Chapter 4. However, Aerospike also supports operations on the map values as well as the map keys.

Consider a use case where you want to be able to operate on the timestamp of the transactions, as in the earlier section, but also want to be able to get transactions that meet a certain dollar amount threshold. So you want to be able to answer, "get any transactions whose dollar amount is greater than or equal to $50,000," for example.

If you look closely at the structure of the preceding data, you will see that the dollar amount is the first value in the list of transaction details:

```
txns: {
        1680113831954: [10000, "New car tire", "txn1"],
        1699422631954: [500, "Ice cream", "txn2"],
        1704423453345: [2750, "Pizza", "txn3"],
        ...
}
```

This means that the "Value" type operations will act on the transaction amount first. To satisfy the preceding query you could do something like:

```
Record record = client.operate(null, key,
    MapOperation.getByValueRange(
        "txns",
        Value.get(Arrays.asList(50000)),
        Value.get(Arrays.asList(Long.MAX_VALUE)),
        MapReturnType.KEY_VALUE));
```

This is very similar to the getByKeyRange call you saw earlier except that it's now operating on the value instead of the key. This will return the keys and values of the records whose amount is greater than the passed values.

Did you notice that the code didn't just pass Value.get(50000) as the starting value but rather Value.get(Arrays.asList(50000))? This is necessary because the value is a list. If you were just to pass Value.get(50000), Aerospike would look at the value you passed (an integer) and compare it to its stored value (a list). Integers are always considered less than a list, so both the start and end values would be less than every list, resulting in no transactions being returned.

However, since the code wrapped the 50,000 in a Java list, Aerospike will compare two lists. As mentioned in "List ordering" on page 109, this will cause Aerospike to look at each item in the list in turn, starting with the first one, the amount. This will yield the desired result.

Associating Objects

You have seen the power of embedding aggregated objects into the parent object, and this is a very common use case. Another common use case is having two top-level objects that refer to one another. For example, a Customer may have multiple Accounts, and Accounts may have multiple Customers. Both are top-level entities that have business value in their own right.

The most common way of handling this is for the Customer object to have a list of Account IDs, and the Accounts object to have a list of the Customer IDs. Figure 6-5 shows the relationships between Customers and Accounts. The Customer IDs associated with that Account are placed in the Account's `custId` list, and the Account IDs are placed in the Customer's `accountIds` list.

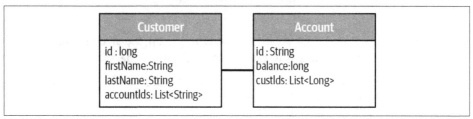

Figure 6-5. Simple relationship between Customers and Accounts

This pattern facilitates navigation from either the Account to the Customer or from the Customer to the Account. If a use case does not require this bidirectional navigation, but the Accounts are always looked up from the Customer, for example, only one list needs to be maintained (the Account IDs in the Customer in this case).

Updating Relationships

Here is an example of creating a relationship between a Customer and an Account. This assumes that both objects have been saved into Aerospike and this code merely links between them in the database:

```
ListPolicy listPolicy = new ListPolicy(
        ListOrder.UNORDERED,
        ListWriteFlags.ADD_UNIQUE | ListWriteFlags.NO_FAIL);

// Put the ID of the account into the customer id list, ignoring duplicates
client.operate(null, new Key(NAMESPACE, CUST_SET, customer.getId()),
    ListOperation.append(listPolicy, "accountIds",
        Value.get(account.getId())));

// Put the ID of the customer into the account id list, ignoring duplicates
client.operate(null, new Key(NAMESPACE, ACCOUNT_SET, account.getId()),
    ListOperation.append(listPolicy, "custIds",
        Value.get(customer.getId())));
```

The code first sets up a `ListPolicy` for the operations. It's important to ensure that the list of IDs contains no duplicates, even if the same account is linked to the same customer multiple times. The `ListWriteFlags.ADD_UNIQUE` flag is used to do this, which will ensure that Aerospike will only put the item in the list if it's not already there. If the item already exists in the list an exception will be thrown. However, in this case, it's desirable to not throw an exception but rather just fail silently, so the

`ListWriteFlags.NO_FAIL` flag is included. This makes the list act as a set of unique values, containing at most one copy of any given ID.

Once this `ListPolicy` has been set up, the ID of the account is placed in the `account Ids` list in the customer record. Since the behavior of the append has been set up by creating the `ListPolicy`, all you have to do is invoke append with the appropriate arguments.

Finally, the customer ID is placed in the `custIds` list on the Account object, very similar to the way the `accountIds` were using the following code:

```
// Put the ID of the customer into the account id list, ignoring duplicates
client.operate(null, new Key(NAMESPACE, ACCOUNT_SET, account.getId()),
    ListOperation.append(listPolicy, "custIds",
        Value.get(customer.getId()))));
```

Some sample data in the database might look like:

```
aql> select * from test.customers
+-----------+-----------+------------------------------------------+
| firstName | lastName  | accountIds                               |
+-----------+-----------+------------------------------------------+
| "Fred"    | "Black"   | LIST('["ACCT-2"]')                       |
| "Bob"     | "Smith"   | LIST('["ACCT-2", "ACCT-5", "ACCT-6"]')   |
...
+-----------+-----------+------------------------------------------+
aql> select * from test.accts
+---------+-------------------+
| balance | custIds           |
+---------+-------------------+
| 600     | LIST('[5]')       |
| 200     | LIST('[2, 3, 5]') |
...
+---------+-------------------+
```

Note that there are two distinct operations here, one on the customer and one on the account. These records are independent records, so there is no transactionality across the two operations, potentially leading to an inconsistent database state if errors occur. At the time of writing, current versions of Aerospike only have transactionality on a single record, but in some cases ordering operations appropriately can be used to work around this. In this example, however, this is not possible. Aerospike version 8 is anticipated to have multirecord transactions, which will solve this problem.

Reading Related Objects

Now that you've got relationships in the database between the objects, you need to be able to read the data back. Note that Aerospike does not support joins like a relational database does, so you will need to use a couple of operations to retrieve the data.

Example 6-1 will assume that you have a customer ID and you want to get all the accounts associated with that customer.

Example 6-1. Retrieving all accounts for a given customer

```java
public List<Account> getAccountsForCustomer(long customerId) {
    List<Account> results = new ArrayList<>();
    Record custRecord = client.get(null,
        new Key(NAMESPACE, CUST_SET, customer.getId(), "accountIds"));
    if (custRecord == null) {
        return results;
    }
    List<String> accountIds = (List<String>)
        custRecord.getList("accountIds");
    Key[] keys = new Key[accountIds.size()];
    for (int i = 0; i < accountIds.size(); i++) {
        keys[i] = new Key(NAMESPACE, ACCOUNT_SET, accountIds.get(i));
    }
    Record[] accounts = client.get(null, keys);
    for (int i = 0; i < accountIds.size(); i++) {
        Record account = accounts[i];
        results.add(new Account(accountIds.get(i),
            account.getLong("balance"),
            (List<Long>)account.getList("custIds")));
    }
    return results;
}
```

The code in Example 6-1 can be broken down into several steps. First, you need to get the list of account IDs from the customer record by performing a simple get on the customer record. However, you only need the list of `accountIds`, not the full customer record, so this bin is listed as the only bin to be retrieved from the `get`:

```java
Record custRecord = client.get(null,
    new Key(NAMESPACE, CUST_SET, customer.getId(), "accountIds"));
```

Aerospike will still read the full customer record from storage but will transmit only the one bin that is needed back to the application. You can omit this step if you already have the full Customer object loaded, as you already have the list of `accountIds`.

Next, you need to iterate through the list of `accountIds`, forming a key to the account record for each of the IDs:

```java
Key[] keys = new Key[accountIds.size()];
for (int i = 0; i < accountIds.size(); i++) {
    keys[i] = new Key(NAMESPACE, ACCOUNT_SET, accountIds.get(i));
}
```

This gives an array of keys, so all that remains is to perform a batch get on these keys and iterate through the results, turning each Aerospike `Record` into an appropriate `Account`:

```
Record[] accounts = client.get(null, keys);
for (int i = 0; i < accountIds.size(); i++) {
    Record account = accounts[i];
    results.add(new Account(accountIds.get(i),
        account.getLong("balance"),
        (List<Long>)account.getList("custIds")));
}
```

This is a very quick way to effectively resolve a one-to-many relationship without needing to do a join.

Storing of IDs

If you look closely at the code where you turn the list of Aerospike records back into Account objects in the previous section, you will notice that the account balance and list of `custIds` come from the Aerospike record, but the ID of the account comes from the list of the `accountIds` retrieved in Example 6-1. Why not just get it out of the record like the other bins? The answer is because, by default, Aerospike *does not store the primary key for a record*!

If you're used to relational databases, this seems like an astounding statement. Surely every record in the database needs to know its PK, otherwise, how can the database select the correct record?

Well, as was mentioned in Chapter 5, the storage and retrieval of the records in Aerospike is done by the digest, the 20-byte hash of the set name and PK. Aerospike stores the digest for each record in lieu of the actual PK. These digests are unique, so they can serve as a PK.

When you think about the applications you've written, how many times have you actually needed the database to tell you what the PK of a record is, except for maybe using them in joins? Almost all the time, you know the PK of the record and you pass this PK to the database when reading it. Consider Example 6-1, which starts with a customer ID. How would you discover the customer ID if it's not stored in the database?

Most applications would allow the user to search for a customer by name, date of birth, or some other criteria. Hence the person using the application would load the Customer object by selecting from a list of customers or similar records. This selection of the customer would be done using the digest, which is returned when forming the list. If the user does provide a `customerId`, this can be used to retrieve the record directly.

In fact, the number of use cases where you actually need to store the ID of a record is very small. Most of the time, you already have the ID to retrieve the object, as the preceding code did when loading the accounts.

What if you do need to store the ID? Well, there are two options for doing so:

1. Manually store the ID explicitly in its own bin.
2. Tell Aerospike to store the ID for you.

The first option is the simplest, but you have to store and read an extra bin.

The second option requires setting a policy value whenever you write the record, passing sendKey = true. For example:

```
WritePolicy writePolicy = new WritePolicy(client.getWritePolicyDefault());
writePolicy.sendKey = true;
client.put(writePolicy, customer.getKey(),
        new Bin("firstName", customer.getFirstName()),
        new Bin("lastName", customer.getLastName()),
        new Bin("accountIds", customer.getAccountIds()));
```

This will pass the PK as well as the digest to the Aerospike server. Aerospike will store the key associated with the record but will also perform an additional check to ensure that the key stored with the record is the same as the passed key. For example, assume the keys "123" and "456" hash to the same digest in a particular set, and that the "123" key was used to write a record. The application then tries to write record "456," which should be a different record. However, it hashes to the same value as "123." If sendKey = false, the write will succeed, overwriting the existing record. However, if sendKey = true on both writes, Aerospike will compare "123" to "456" and throw an exception because they're different, meaning that they're different records.

Hence, if you're worried about hash collisions on the digest, this technique safeguards against it. However, the probability of two different keys hashing to the same value is infinitesimally small; mankind knows of no two values that hash to the same digest. Note that using sendKey = true will force a read of the record from storage to retrieve the actual PK even on write operations, potentially introducing additional latency. You can use aql to see what happens when you send the key:

```
aql> set key_send false
KEY_SEND = false
aql> insert into test.newSet(pk, value) values (1, 1)
OK, 1 record affected.
aql> select * from test.newSet
+-------+
| value |
+-------+
|   1   |
+-------+
1 row in set (0.173 secs)
```

```
OK
aql> set key_send true
KEY_SEND = true
aql> insert into test.newSet(pk, value) values (1, 1)
OK, 1 record affected.
aql> select * from test.newSet
+----+-------+
| PK | value |
+----+-------+
| 1  | 1     |
+----+-------+
1 row in set (0.154 secs)
OK
```

 AQL uses key_send to send the key; Java uses sendKey—same idea but different naming. Also, AQL defaults key_send to true, but the Aerospike clients default it to false. This typically isn't an issue as data in production systems is only inserted via the application, not through AQL.

As you can see, when you set key_send to false, Aerospike can only return the value bin even though all columns were requested. Once key_send is set to true and the record reinserted, Aerospike can return the key of the record.

Other Common Data Modeling Problems

Let's turn to a set of problems that crop up regularly and look at solutions to them. As with many data modeling problems, there can be more than one correct solution, and each use case tends to put its own nuances on the problem.

External ID Resolution

Companies frequently share information with partners these days and it is not uncommon for a record created with internal data to be augmented with data from external sources for data enrichment purposes. This is particularly prevalent in the Advertising Technology vertical, for example. These external data sources can also request the information back, augmented with information from the internal source too.

For example, Company A stores a list of topics they think a person may be interested in, called "audience segments." So they might know that Bob is interested in "sports," for example, and have a record with key 1234 holding this information. They then receive some audience segmentation data from Company B, and they work out that this data also contains audience segments for Bob. However, the key that Company B uses for Bob is 6789. Company A merges the audience segments from Company B into its record of 1234, but they have to know that when Company B asks for 6789, they have to return the record they know as 1234.

So the internal ID of 1234 sometimes needs to be discovered using an external ID of 6789. The obvious way to do this is using a secondary index with a structure like:

PK	external_id	data
1234	6789	{...}

A secondary index on `external_id` could be defined so that when the external ID is provided, a secondary index query is performed, looking for the record that matches the passed ID.

However, this is not a good use of secondary indexes. The external ID is assumed to be unique, so looking up data matching the external ID will yield either no records or one record. Remember that secondary index queries are "scatter-gather," so a request will be sent to every node in the cluster, looking for matching records on that node. The client has to coordinate requests to multiple server nodes and every server node will do work looking for that external ID, with potentially only one finding the record.

Worse, as the cluster scales, say from 10 nodes to 20 nodes, the amount of work the cluster performs increases (doubles in this case) while returning exactly the same result. This is *inversely scalable*—definitely not ideal.

A better way of solving this problem is as follows: have one set which maps external IDs to internal IDs, and another set that has the internal ID mapped to the data, as shown in Figure 6-6.

PK	Internal_id		PK	Data
6789	1234	→	1234	{...}

Figure 6-6. External ID lookup resolving to an internal key

When an external ID comes into the system, two key-value reads are performed: one to read the external ID and retrieve the internal ID, and the other one to read the data associated with that ID. So the code might resemble:

```
Record record = client.get(null, new Key("test", "extId", 6789));
if (record != null) {
    record = client.get(null, new Key("test", "data",
                        record.getLong("internal_id")));
}
```

Key-value reads are incredibly efficient in Aerospike due to the HMA covered in Chapter 5, so these two reads will likely be finished in a millisecond or two depending on the hardware the cluster runs on.

If you're used to relational databases, performing two operations is typically frowned upon, with a preference for one more complex operation. However, with Aerospike, simpler operations are so quick and efficient that it is a very common technique.

The Very Small Object Problem

The preceding technique with two key-value lookups is very efficient and solves the internal/external index problem very nicely. However, it does suffer from one drawback: each copy of each record in Aerospike requires 64 bytes for the primary index, which is normally held in memory (RAM). For larger records this is typically not an issue, but here our objects contain just two IDs, meaning that the data is possibly even smaller than the RAM needed for the primary index.

One way around this is to merge multiple records into a single record using a map. This assumes you have some knowledge about the distribution of keys. For the sake of this example, assume the external IDs are 10-digit numbers, randomly distributed over the whole range, and there are a billion of these external IDs.

If each external ID to internal ID is mapped as a single record and Aerospike has been configured to store two copies of each record, the RAM requirements across the cluster will be:

64 bytes × 2 copies × 1,000,000,000 records ~= 128 GB

128 GB across the cluster might not seem like much on modern machines, but remember that this is just for one small component of this use case. This lowers the system resources left for other database records.

Merging multiple of these small records into one big record is easy. Diagrammatically, what you want to do is shown in Figure 6-7.

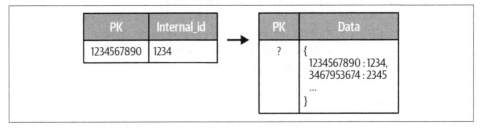

Figure 6-7. Merging internal/external ID key values into a single map bin

So the 10-digit external ID goes from being the PK of a record to being a map key, with the internal ID being the map value. There will be multiple records containing these maps as a billion entries will not fit into a single map, so the question is: given an external ID, what PK should be used to store or read that external ID from the map?

A good way of working this out is deciding how big you want the records holding the maps to be. Normally a few kilobytes is a good size; it's not too heavy on the SSDs when being read or written and gives a reasonable ratio of primary index RAM (64 bytes) to actual storage. In this example, the combination of the external ID and internal ID is small, potentially about 50 bytes.

So, if the desired record size is about 4 kilobytes and each record is 50 bytes, that would lead to an optimal size of (4,000/50) entries in each map record, or around 80. However, it doesn't matter if it's a bit more or bit less than this; it's an approximate order of magnitude.

What if you took the external ID and dropped the last three digits, so a key of 123,456 became 123? Would this form a good unique PK? It would certainly result in multiple external IDs mapping to the same PK, as all the numbers between 123,000 and 123,999 would map to the same PK: 123.

The worst case is there are a thousand entries in one of the maps, but the external IDs are random, so this is very unlikely to occur. A 10-digit number yields 10 billion possible numbers and 1 billion of them have been used, so on average, each map will hold around a hundred entries—one-tenth of the thousand you divided the external ID by. To continue the example of the thousand keys between 123,000 and 123,999, statistically only 100 of them will likely be used.

This gives a very simple algorithm to save and retrieve these IDs:

```
private Key getKey(long externalId) {
    return new Key("test", "mapping", externalId / 1000);
}

public void saveMapping(long externalId, long internalId) {
    client.operate(null, getKey(externalId),
        MapOperation.put(MapPolicy.Default, "map",
            Value.get(externalId), Value.get(internalId)));
}

public long getInternalId(long externalId) {
    Record record = client.operate(null, getKey(externalId),
        MapOperation.getByKey("map",
            Value.get(externalId), MapReturnType.VALUE));
    if (record != null) {
        return record.getLong("map");
    }
    return 0;
}
```

The key is determined by taking the external ID and dividing by a thousand. To save a mapping from an external ID to an internal ID, you use the `MapOpera tion.put(...)` operation, and to retrieve the internal ID from an external ID, you use the `MapOperation.get(...)` operation.

This algorithm works well and is simple to use and understand. There is one refinement you could make. Every map key in one map is identical except for the last three digits. You know this because the record key is the external ID (the map key) divided by a thousand. Instead of storing the whole external ID in the map each time, you could just store the last three digits. This would optimize space in the database, and the only changes to the preceding code would be changing both occurrences of `Value.get(externalId)` to `Value.get(externalId%1000)`.

What if your keys aren't numbers or their randomness is not great? Then hash the keys using a good hashing algorithm like RIPEMD160 or similar, and take a set of bits from the hash, which gives a number greater than the anticipated number of keys.

Expiry of Map Entries

The last problem to examine is common in several verticals: information is stored in a map and the information has an expiration date after which that information is not useful and can be removed. Aerospike supports automatic removal of records based on a TTL, but not automatic expiry of map entries.

To develop expiry of map entries, you will need a map that contains the information, including the expiry time of the information in the map entry. The value in the map will be a list containing this expiry time as the first item, followed by other pertinent information. For example, an ad-tech use case is audience segmentation, as discussed before. For a particular device (phone, tablet, etc.) a list of segments (interests) is stored. These segments show topics that you may have browsed recently, and hence might be interested in finding out more information about, meaning that showing you an ad related to these segments might be more impactful.

Any segments not seen in the last 30 days are considered irrelevant to your current interests and should be removed from the map. So a sample record might look like:

```
segments: {
    "CRICKET":  [1680243671492, "icc-cricket.com"],
    "DATABASE": [1680243859728, "aerospike.com"],
    "KUNG_FU":  [1680243656968, "shaolin.com"]
}
```

In this case there are three segments in the map for this device. Each segment has a name (the map key), an expiry time (first element in the list of values), and an originating source—the website that reported the interest in the segment. This is obviously a simplified example but serves for illustrative purposes.

Three operations need to be performed on this data:

1. Retrieving any segments that have not expired (so that the expiry date is in the future)

2. Adding a new segment with its expiry date

3. Removing any segments that have expired

Retrieve any active segments

Perhaps you want to get any elements from the map whose expiry time is in the future. You can use the getByValueRange operation for this, similar to how it was used earlier in the chapter to get the list of credit card transactions that were active:

```
Date now = new Date().getTime();
Record record = client.operate(writePolicy, key,
    MapOperation.getByValueRange("segments",
        Value.get(Arrays.asList(now)), Value.INFINITY,
        MapReturnType.KEY));
```

The parameters to the getByValueRange call are the bin name (segments), the start time (now, but as a list), the end time (INFINITY), and the information to be returned, in this case just the key (the segment name). If a segment is valid, the expiry time will be in the future and these parameters select these entries. For this dataset, the result will be a List containing [CRICKET, DATABASE, KUNG_FU].

Adding new segments and removing expired segments

Adding a new segment just requires forming the list containing the expiry date and the values and inserting the entries into the map. This is the code to do that:

```
long now = new Date().getTime();
long expiryMs = now + MS_IN_30_DAYS; // Add 30 days
List<Object> data = Arrays.asList(expiryMs, "pi.com");
client.operate(writePolicy, key,
    MapOperation.removeByValueRange("segments",
        Value.get(Arrays.asList(0)),
        Value.get(Arrays.asList(now)),
        MapReturnType.NONE),
    MapOperation.put(MapPolicy.Default, "segments",
        Value.get("ELECTRONICS"), Value.get(data)));
```

Note that there are two operations in the operate call: one to add the new entry (a list of Objects) into the map with MapOperation.put and another to remove any expired segments with MapOperation.removeByValueRange. removeByValueRange is done first, throwing away any elements whose timestamp is in the range of zero to the current time. As the timestamp being stored is an expiry epoch, having an expiry time in the past means that entry is expired.

Once the expired values have been removed, the put places the new values into the map. Note that if the segment already exists in the map, the new value will overwrite the old one, updating the expiry time to the new time as would be expected in this use case.

The removal of the elements being done at the same time as adding a new element is fairly efficient. The record has been read from storage and will need to be written back to storage anyway, so removing the extra elements incurs no extra storage accesses. However, removeByValueRange will require the map to be sorted if it has been set up as a KEY_ORDERED map, which does have some CPU cost.

If you're calling this method at a moderate frequency, this extra CPU cost is unlikely to make a difference. Aerospike is normally very light on CPU, so the database nodes normally have spare CPU cycles. However, if you're calling this method very quickly, this might become an issue. If it does there are two simple solutions:

1. Version 7 of Aerospike looks set to allow maps created as KEY_VALUE_ORDERED to optionally save the value-ordered index to storage along with the record. This will remove the CPU cost of a full sort, but at the cost of extra storage space for the index.

2. Instead of performing the removeByValue range on every call, defer it to a background query operation running at a controlled requests per second rate, limiting the impact on the cluster. If the map contains some entries that have expired for an extra period of time, it will not impact the functionality of the other operations.

Summary

Data modeling is crucial to efficiently using any database and Aerospike is no exception. You must take care to ensure the implementation of a good data model that solves the business problem. Not only should the right data model perform well, but it should typically also reduce the amount of hardware required to solve the problem.

Like most data modeling problems, there are multiple ways to solve the same problem. The techniques in this chapter have given you a brief introduction to some ways of solving the business problem, but they are certainly not comprehensive. A comprehensive look at data modeling in Aerospike would take a whole book all by itself, but hopefully these building blocks give you enough to go on to begin modeling for your use cases.

In the next chapter, you'll start to learn about configuring and administering Aerospike.

## CHAPTER 7

Administration, Tools, and Configuration

Now that you're ready to bring an Aerospike cluster online, you need to know how to keep the system online and deal with changes. You should understand the processes used to interact with the server so that you can manage it as part of your production environment. You will need to know how to cluster servers together, tune parameters, and manage user access. This chapter focuses on these essential aspects of administering Aerospike, exploring the tools and configurations to manage your Aerospike clusters.

Configuration

With your Aerospike installation, a configuration file should have been created at */etc/aerospike/aerospike.conf*. This is the main configuration file and is only read when the Aerospike daemon is started. The format of this file does not adhere to any specific configuration formats such as YAML, JSON, or even INI. The format is proprietary and specific to Aerospike, though it resembles JSON.

Anatomy of a Config File

The Aerospike config file is divided into various sections known as *contexts* and *subcontexts*. Comments in the config file can be added by prepending the # symbol. You can use the Aerospike configuration reference (*https://oreil.ly/NCcMt*) to determine what each parameter does, review additional notes, and see properties of that configuration parameter, which will be discussed soon.

We strongly recommend that you bookmark the Aerospike configuration reference (*https://oreil.ly/TgxzF*). It's an invaluable resource for interpreting the book and will prove useful in your day-to-day activities with Aerospike, as well as for infrequent reference needs. The config reference guide will be your go-to source for navigating and understanding Aerospike's configurations effectively.

Let's start by examining a skeleton of the config file with no values (Example 7-1). This skeleton is provided directly from Aerospike's configuration documentation (*https://oreil.ly/f9s3h*) and briefly explains each context section. You should not copy this file, as it is not a working example.

Example 7-1. The Aerospike server configuration file skeleton

```
service {} # Tuning parameters, process owner, feature
# key file

network { # Used to configure intracluster and
    # application-node communications
    service {} # Tools/Application communications protocol
    fabric {} # Intracluster communications protocol
    info {} # Administrator telnet console protocol
    heartbeat {} # Cluster formation protocol
 }

security { # (Optional, Enterprise Edition only) to enable
# access control on the cluster
}

logging {} # Logging configuration

xdr { # (Optional, Enterprise Edition only) Configure
# Cross-Datacenter Replication
}

namespace { # Define namespace record policies and storage
    # engine
    storage-engine {} # Configure persistence or lack of persistence
    set {} # (Optional) Set specific record policies
}

mod-lua { # location of UDF modules
}
```

The skeleton is useful as it helps show the overall structure of the configuration file, but since it isn't an actual configuration file, it's hard to conceptually think about what should fill out the empty sections.

Let's examine a real functional configuration file that ships with an Aerospike installation. For this example, the enterprise server package for Aerospike v6.3 is downloaded to target the Ubuntu operating system (see Example 7-2). The config file should rarely change between Aerospike versions and Linux distributions, so this example should be virtually identical, regardless of your operating system or version.

Example 7-2. Default Aerospike configuration file

```
# Aerospike database configuration file for use with systemd.

service {
        proto-fd-max 15000
}

logging {
        console {
                context any info
        }
}

network {
        service {
                address any
                port 3000
        }

        heartbeat {
                mode multicast
                multicast-group 239.1.99.222
                port 9918
                # To use unicast-mesh heartbeats, remove the 3 lines above, and see
                # aerospike_mesh.conf for alternative.
                interval 150
                timeout 10
        }
        fabric {
                port 3001
        }
        info {
                port 3003
        }
}

namespace test {
        replication-factor 2
        memory-size 4G
        storage-engine memory
}

namespace bar {
```

```
        replication-factor 2
        memory-size 4G
        storage-engine memory
        # To use file storage backing, comment out the line above and use the
        # following lines instead.
#       storage-engine device {
#               file /opt/aerospike/data/bar.dat
#               filesize 16G
#               data-in-memory true # Store data in memory in addition to file.
#       }
}
```

Service context

The first context in the config file is the `service` context. The `service` context allows you to specify settings for high-level daemon-related runtime parameters that you can find using the configuration reference. You can safely assume the default values in the file are reasonable for most deployments to start, and change them later if needed:

```
service {
    proto-fd-max 15000
}
```

The first value you'll see is a configuration parameter called `proto-fd-max` with a value of 15000. `proto-fd-max` is a parameter that controls the maximum number of open file descriptors (fd) opened on behalf of client connections. Refer to the configuration reference (*https://oreil.ly/ZUUz4*) for more information.

Logging context

The second setting is for the vital `logging` context. This controls where Aerospike stores logs:

```
logging {
    console {
        context any info
    }
}
```

By default, logging messages are stored in the console, stdout. Console logs can be retrieved using the `docker logs` command if you are using Aerospike with Docker. If not, use:

```
journalctl -u aerospike.service
```

The major customizations you can change in the logging context are:

- Logging to a file additionally, or instead of, the console
- Using the syslog
- Splitting specific messages into separate log locations

 In some scenarios you may be restarting the daemon and it does not start or produce logs. This usually happens because the configuration file was invalid, so the logs did not go to where you expected. If you cannot find log entries in your specified location you may need to consider running the */usr/bin/asd* (location may vary) binary directly, which will print the error directly to your console.

Network context

The following is the network context with subcontexts of service, heartbeat, fabric, and info:

```
network {
    service {
        address any
        port 3000
    }

    heartbeat {
        mode multicast
        multicast-group 239.1.99.222
        port 9918
        interval 150
        timeout 10
    }

    fabric {
        port 3001
    }

    info {
        port 3003
    }
}
```

Under the network context, the service context shows that Aerospike will be listening on all IP addresses on the machine, and that clients will connect on port 3000.

The `heartbeat` context here is how you configure Aerospike's clustering strategy. In this example, `multicast` is being used, where each server sends a broadcast to form a cluster within the multicast group.

The broadcast is configured to be sent to `239.1.99.222` on port 9918. The `interval` and `timeout` parameters control the threshold at which Aerospike will consider a server to be unreachable. A timeout value of 10 means that 10 heartbeats will have to fail consecutively before a server is considered to no longer be part of the cluster. The heartbeat is sent on a schedule controlled by the interval setting, which is configured as 150 milliseconds. If a server becomes unreachable for some reason, the remaining nodes in the cluster will take timeout × interval, 150 ms × 10, or about 1.5 seconds, to recognize that.

In some environments, especially cloud, multicast is not available. Use mesh mode for clustering on platforms where multicast is unavailable or not desired. You can follow the guide on configuring heartbeat (*https://oreil.ly/maiyv*) in the Aerospike documentation.

If you are using mesh, the heartbeat section will look similar to the following, where the mode is set to `mesh` and a list of IPs to cluster to is provided:

```
heartbeat {
        mode mesh
        mesh-seed-address-port 10.0.0.123 3002
        mesh-seed-address-port 10.0.0.124 3002
        mesh-seed-address-port 10.0.0.125 3002
        port 3002
        interval 150
        timeout 10
}
```

Each entry of `mesh-seed-address-port` will tell Aerospike to try to cluster with a node at that address. So in this configuration the machine will try to cluster with machines at `10.0.0.123`, `10.0.0.124`, and `10.0.0.125`.

> It is not necessary to omit the node's own IP address from this list. For example, if deployed on a machine with the IP `10.0.0.124`, you do not need to omit `mesh-seed-address-port 10.0.0.124 3002` from the configuration file. This is nice in case you want to have identical config files on all nodes in your cluster.

Continuing our review of Example 7-2, the `fabric` subcontext controls the communication between the Aerospike servers in the cluster for replication and data redistribution, which will happen over port 3001:

```
fabric {
  port 3001
}
```

The info context follows immediately and controls the *info protocol:*

```
info {
  port 3003
}
```

Administrative tools use the info protocol to communicate to a running server, for things like dynamic configuration and fetching runtime statistics. This configures the info protocol to communicate over port 3003. You shouldn't need to modify many other parameters in either the fabric or info contexts, but the available options can be found in the configuration reference (*https://oreil.ly/8s6IV*).

Namespace context

The namespace contexts are another important configuration area to explore. This is where you define what namespaces the server will make available and what properties they have:

```
namespace test {
    replication-factor 2
    memory-size 4G
    storage-engine memory
}
```

The first defined namespace is called test. It has a replication-factor of 2, which means that Aerospike will store one replica copy of every record. You can see the memory-size parameter is specified as 4G, limiting the size of the combination of the index and data stored to less than 4 GiB.

 Unless otherwise specified, all space-related parameters in Aerospike are binary representations of their unit. 1G means 1 gibibyte, not 1 gigabyte. A gibibyte is 1,024 mebibytes or 2^{30} bytes. This may confuse an operator because some hardware information references of resources may show units in GB. If some resource shows 500 GB as available memory, that only equals 465 G in Aerospike as it is 465 GiB of memory. Most size-related parameters support some short form of units like this, and you should consult the configuration reference.

Finally, in the last context shown in Example 7-2 you will find the storage-engine parameter, which uses memory as the storage-engine for the first namespace. The stock configuration also includes a configuration for a second namespace definition, bar:

```
namespace bar {
    replication-factor 2
    memory-size 4G
    storage-engine memory

    # To use file storage backing, comment out the line above and use the
    # following lines instead.
#    storage-engine device {
#        file /opt/aerospike/data/bar.dat
#        filesize 16G
#        data-in-memory true # Store data in memory in addition to file.
#    }
}
```

 The replication-factor can be a confusing topic semantically. Think of it as "how many times Aerospike will store the data" instead of using words like replication, master, and copy. A replication-factor of 2 means Aerospike will have a master and a replica. A replication-factor of 1 means Aerospike will store only a master record. A replication-factor of 3 means a master record and two replica copies will be stored. In most cases the recommended value is a replication-factor of 2, which allows the Aerospike cluster to lose one server (or one rack if using the rack-aware property) in a cluster with no data loss.

The bar namespace uses memory as its storage-engine, but you can see another type of storage-engine commented out. Let's briefly cover the various storage-engine options more in depth as this is another key configuration parameter.

There are three storage-engines available using Aerospike: memory, device, and Intel's Persistent Memory (PMem). Aerospike's most popular storage-engine is device. Using the device storage-engine makes Aerospike store the data in a storage device while having the index in-memory. This hybrid configuration of maintaining the index in-memory and storing data on device is usually the most appealing of various trade-offs. Table 7-1 summarizes some high-level trade-offs made when picking a storage-engine.

Table 7-1. storage-engine trade-off matrix (source: Aerospike documentation (https://oreil.ly/Puv22))

storage-engine	Hybrid/Device (data not in memory)	All Flash	Device (data in memory)	Memory Only (no persistence)	Persistent Memory***
Index in Memory	✓		✓	✓	✓
Fast Restart	✓	✓	✓		✓
Survive a Power Outage	✓	✓	✓		✓

As you can see in Table 7-1, the index can also be moved out of memory into PMem or flash. The "All Flash" configuration stores the index on SSD to maximize keyspace at the cost of performance, by moving the primary index into a flash device instead of storing the primary index in memory.

 As of January 31, 2023, Intel Intel canceled and ceased development on Optane products such as Optane PMem and Optane SSD.

The Fast Restart referenced in Table 7-1 is an Aerospike Enterprise Edition–only feature. Fast Restart allows the restarting of an Aerospike daemon that uses a device-backed namespace without having to rebuild the primary index. When the index is lost, Aerospike must scan the storage devices to rebuild the primary index from the persisted data.

 The default configuration that ships with the Aerospike server is designed to be compatible with most systems but makes one notable performance trade-off for that compatibility: it uses the `file` `storage-engine` subcontext. One of Aerospike's strengths is that it can utilize the raw direct devices without a filesystem, but this can be challenging for first-time users to configure. If you plan a production deployment, consider using devices instead of files with Aerospike's `storage-engine`.

Dynamic Configuration

Many of the parameters in the reference guide (*https://oreil.ly/6Z-Zw*) can be changed dynamically without downtime, but some have special requirements. The configuration reference guide includes a legend, shown in Figure 7-1, indicating if that parameter needs to be set on restart or can be set dynamically, etc., which is referred to as the *configuration parameter's property*. For example, the *context* parameter is a dynamic property, and if you highlight over this legend, you can see it explains it can be set dynamically.

By understanding what a configuration parameter does and under what circumstances it can be changed, you can manage your configuration more effectively. Table 7-2 summarizes the various properties of the configuration parameters in a table.

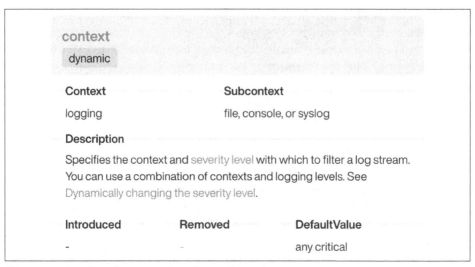

context	
dynamic	
Context	**Subcontext**
logging	file, console, or syslog
Description	

Specifies the context and severity level with which to filter a log stream. You can use a combination of contexts and logging levels. See Dynamically changing the severity level.

Introduced	**Removed**	**DefaultValue**
-	-	any critical

Figure 7-1. Reading the properties of a configuration parameter

Table 7-2. Configuration parameter properties

Configuration property	Meaning
dynamic	This configuration parameter can be changed on the running server without requiring a restart.
static	Static configuration parameters can only be changed with a server restart. You must update the configuration file and restart the Aerospike daemon.
unanimous	The configuration parameter must have the same value on all nodes across the cluster. Changing these values may require a total cluster downtime or special procedure to change. Nodes that disagree on a unanimous parameter will be prevented from joining the cluster on startup.
enterprise	These parameters require an Aerospike Enterprise Edition license to use.
required	Aerospike will fail to start if a required parameter is not specified. A log entry should be generated.

 Dynamic configuration is a powerful tool with a potentially nasty drawback: there is no way to flush the changes back to the configuration file. If you made dynamic changes to the Aerospike server while it was running, they will be lost unless you also write them to the configuration file. The configuration file is the only source of configuration during a startup. There is no method to print a diff of runtime configuration versus the static configuration file, or a way to copy runtime configuration to a file. Each time you make a dynamic change, you should manually add it to the config file if you intend for it to survive upgrades. asadm has a show config diff command that may help identify these.

Now that you know how to read the reference manual for configuring Aerospike, how do you make and see those dynamic changes? You need to familiarize yourself with the tools package and how to interact with Aerospike before you get started with tuning parameters dynamically, or inspecting current runtime values.

Tools

Your Aerospike installation should have included a tools package with it, and if not you can follow the steps outlined in Chapter 2 to get those set up. The tools package provides executable programs to manage your Aerospike installation once it's online. Let's start by going over a cursory summary of all the tools provided with a brief explanation of each in Table 7-3 before getting into the details.

Table 7-3. Tools provided to manage Aerospike

Tool	Description
asinfo	Used to execute info commands against one aerospike instance. info commands can retrieve information like latency, statistics, usage. asinfo can also be used to set parameters.
asadm	Used to execute info commands against many Aerospike instances, as well as managing access, secondary indexes, and *user-defined functions* (UDFs).
aql	Aerospike Quick Look, AQL, is used to perform some basic CRUD operations against a server without needing to write a full program.
asbackup and asrestore	Used to take and restore full, incremental, or partial backups of a running cluster.
asloglatency	Used to inspect the latency of various histograms by reading the logfile.
asbench	Used to simulate various workloads against Aerospike for testing.

asinfo

The asinfo tool is used to change an online cluster without causing downtime, to fetch statistics about the running server, and to assist with troubleshooting. The tool's basic usage is asinfo -v <command to run>. There are other options you may want to use like -l to split lines, -U and -P to specify a user and password, and a few others. You can view asinfo's argument help by running asinfo --help.

Dynamic configuration

The most useful feature of asinfo may be that it allows you to easily change dynamic configuration parameters listed in the configuration reference, without affecting the entire cluster. If you think your use case may benefit from modifying some tunable parameter or you're unsure about the impact of what changing a parameter might be, asinfo helps limit the scope a lot by allowing you to easily specify the change only be made on one host, without needing to restart a server.

Let's walk through an example of changing a dynamic configuration. If you open the configuration reference guide (*https://oreil.ly/lUqqi*) and find a parameter tagged as dynamic, you should be able to modify that using `asinfo`. `memory-size` is one that you are likely to have to change frequently, so let's start there. If you don't see the parameter you're searching for when using the config reference, you may need to select `All` versions or `All Fields` in the search box.

When you look up `memory-size` in the configuration reference, you will see it is dynamic and under the namespace context as shown in Figure 7-2. You can change it through `asinfo`, and the statement to change it needs to be scoped to namespace.

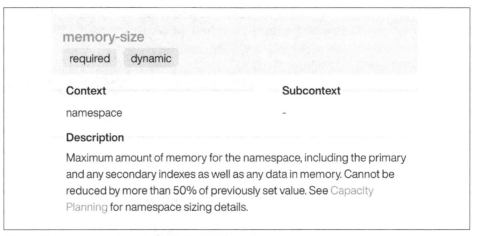

Figure 7-2. memory-size configuration parameter

 There is an "Additional Information" expansion on this reference that shows the command to modify this parameter for a specific namespace. The additional information is usually very helpful, and sometimes it can help get you going faster. Use this to your advantage!

The command to fetch a configuration parameter starts with `get-config`. By default, this command returns the `service` context configuration. You want to fetch a namespace-level configuration though, as this configuration reference tells you `memory-size` is a part of a namespace's configuration. You can do this by specifying the context as namespace, like so:

```
$ asinfo -v 'get-config:context=namespace'
Error::invalid id
```

This returns an error because you can have multiple namespaces. This specific context requires you to append `namespace` with the specific namespace you want. The namespace in this cluster is `test`, so you append `id=test`:

```
$ asinfo -v 'get-config:context=namespace;id=test'
allow-ttl-without-nsup=false;background-query-max-rps=10000;
conflict-resolution-policy=generation;conflict-resolve-writes=false;data-i....
```

That's a lot of information! You can filter this down further by using the -l option to split this into lines and then pipe into grep:

```
$ asinfo -lv 'get-config:context=namespace;id=test'|grep memory
high-water-memory-pct=0
memory-size=1073741824
stop-writes-sys-memory-pct=90
storage-engine.data-in-memory=false
```

If you can write something that succinctly and specifically fetches a parameter, then setting it is a small change. Create a command that fetches the configuration you want, then change the verb from get to set and append the particular config parameter to change. In this way, creating a command that fetches a particular parameter becomes a way to set that parameter. This will help you have confidence in building the command and also check it immediately after.

You can see the memory size here is shown in bytes. 1073741824 is 1 GiB, so our current memory-size set on the namespace is 1 G. You can change this to 2 G by using a similar command, set-config, and adding which parameter must be changed to which value:

```
$ asinfo -v 'set-config:context=namespace;id=test;memory-size=2G'
ok
$ asinfo -lv 'get-config:context=namespace;id=test'|grep memory-size
memory-size=2147483648
```

Similarly, you can read and change the configuration parameters in the service context:

```
$ asinfo -lv 'get-config:context=service'|head
advertise-ipv6=false
auto-pin=none
batch-index-threads=12
batch-max-buffers-per-queue=255
batch-max-requests=5000
batch-max-unused-buffers=256
cluster-name=null
debug-allocations=none
disable-udf-execution=false
downgrading=false
```

Try changing the first configuration parameter you found, `advertise-ipv6`:

```
$ asinfo -lv 'set-config:context=service;advertise-ipv6=true'
ok
$ asinfo -lv 'get-config:context=service'|head -n1
advertise-ipv6=true
```

You can follow this pattern for many of the contexts within the configuration file. If you intend to change this on many servers, you should use `asadm` to make this change instead, which we will cover later in this chapter.

Statistics, special settings, latencies

Separate from the configuration reference that we've focused on so much so far, there is also a reference for info commands (*https://oreil.ly/oT4eU*), which shows the other utilities `asinfo` can help execute. Of special note are the commands `latencies` and `logs`. The `latencies` command allows you to report the last 10 seconds of transactions as a histogram, useful for monitoring. The `logs` command allows you to change the verbosity of various types of messages, such as turning off a particular warning or making some code paths more verbose for troubleshooting. All of the various other ways of using `asinfo` are for more advanced users and situations/problems outside the scope of this book.

> It should be noted that the info command reference guide is a generic reference for the info protocol, and you can execute these commands using the client driver if you need to run these from an application. Aerospike provides all these utilities, but none of them are required. You can re-create the functionality of all of these tools, or some subset of their functionality, in a custom-written application. For example, consider:
>
> ```
> $ asinfo -v 'get-config:context=namespace;id=test'
> ```
>
> This is equivalent to a Java info call:
>
> ```
> Info.request(node, 'get-config:context=namespace;id=test');
> ```

asadm

The `asadm` utility is primarily an info protocol tool like `asinfo`, but for the whole cluster. When you need to check the health of a cluster as a whole, a tool like `asadm` is helpful as it can fetch information from all members of the cluster and summarize them in a readable form. If you need to change a setting across the entire cluster, `asadm` is also the first choice in executing a change like this. `asadm` also enables you to manage access-control lists (ACLs), quotas, secondary indices, and user-defined functions (UDFs).

There are two help commands for asadm. First, passing --help at the command line while executing asadm will give you usage to get connected to the cluster:

```
$ asadm --help
```

The second help command describes which commands you can run from within the asadm shell. When you execute the asadm command, you will enter an asadm interactive session. You can tell you are inside the session because it will prefix the cursor with Admin>. You can run the command help here to see what commands are available, and the exit command to quit the asadm shell:

```
$ asadm
...
Found 1 nodes
Online: 127.0.0.1:3000
Admin>
```

Managing Aerospike will likely start with fetching information and reviewing the cluster. So let's start by covering ways to fetch and visualize information from the cluster.

Informational commands

Once you're inside the asadm interactive shell, info is a great command to start with:

```
Admin> info
```

This command gives you a decent picture of the current state of the cluster: if migrations are pending, how many servers are in the cluster, how many records exist and replicas, how much space is being used, and a few other things. If you execute the help info command, you can see different modifiers, and in the following sections, you can display summaries and statistics on: dc, network, set, sindex, xdr, namespace. These can be added after the info command. For example:

```
Admin> info set
~~~~~~~~~~~~~~~~~~~Set Information (2024-07-07 18:07:23 UTC)~~~~~~~~~~~~~~~~~~
Namespace| Set  |  Node     |Storage |~~Size~~| Total |~Records~|Disable |Set
         |      |           | Engine |~Quota~~|Records|~~Quota~~|Eviction|Index
         |      |           | Used   | Total  |       | Total   |
bar      |myset1|mydc-1:3000|78.047KB| 0.000B |999.000|    0    |False   | No
bar      |myset1|           |78.047KB| 0.000B |999.000|         |        |
bar      |myset2|mydc-1:3000|78.047KB| 0.000B |999.000|    0    |False   | No
bar      |myset2|           |78.047KB| 0.000B |999.000|         |        |
Number of rows: 2
```

This overview of your cluster will be missing the latencies. You can find latency using the show command. The help show command will print the help menu for the available show commands. Some interesting show commands for getting started are show latencies, show statistics, and show config:

```
Admin> show latencies
~~~~~~~~~~~~~~~~~~~~~Latency (2023-08-07 00:10:19 UTC)~~~~~~~~~~~~~~~~~~~~
Namespace|Histogram|                        Node|ops/sec|>1ms|>8ms|>64ms
test     |read     |1.0.0.127.in-addr.arpa:3000 | 2658.6|0.11| 0.0| 0.0
         |         |                            | 2658.6|0.11| 0.0| 0.0
test     |write    |1.0.0.127.in-addr.arpa:3000 | 2650.7|0.11| 0.0| 0.0
         |         |                            | 2650.7|0.11| 0.0| 0.0
Number of rows: 2
Admin>
```

The show latencies command gives us a breakdown of how many reads, writes, UDFs, and batch transactions occurred in the last 10 seconds, as well as what percentage of these transactions fell into various latency buckets.

Another very useful modifier that you can specify with the show command is the like keyword. For example:

```
Admin> show lat like write
```

 You can shorten commands at the expense of readability. Most commands require only enough characters to disambiguate which to execute; for example, if you type s and hit the Tab key twice, you will see that the command s is ambiguous. It could mean either show or summary. If you type su, it is unambiguous enough to execute the closest matching command, which is summary. If you find these shortened forms online in examples and are uncertain what they stand for, you can hit Tab to autocomplete their meaning. For example: i <TAB> will autocomplete to info. Similarly sh la<TAB> will autocomplete to sh latencies.

This view is especially useful when combined with the config section. It differs from executing commands like get-config in asinfo because it can search all config sections from all nodes in the cluster:

```
Admin> sh config like thread
~~~Service Configuration (2023-08-07 00:14:31 UTC)~~~
Node               |1.0.0.127.in-addr.arpa:3000
batch-index-threads|12
info-threads       |16
migrate-threads    |1
query-threads-limit|128
```

As useful as browsing can be, finding an exact parameter name can be challenging. Using the like keyword can help you limit what needs to be viewed to a specific pattern if desired:

```
Admin> sh stat like client.*err
~~~~~Service Statistics (2023-08-07 00:17:32 UTC)~~~~
Node                   |1.0.0.127.in-addr.arpa:3000
early_tsvc_client_error |0
Number of rows: 2

~test Namespace Statistics (2023-08-07 00:17:32 UTC)~
Node                   |1.0.0.127.in-addr.arpa:3000
client_delete_error    |0
client_lang_error      |0
...
```

Finally, the summary command is a great way to summarize a cluster's usage without having to get too technical about all the Aerospike-specific terminology:

```
Admin> summary
~~~~~~~~~~~~~~~~~~Cluster Summary~~~~~~~~~~~~~~~~~~~
Migrations                  |False
Cluster Name                |mydc
Server Version              |C-6.4.0.1,C-6.3.0.25
OS Version                  |--
Cluster Size                |3
Devices Total               |0
Devices Per-Node            |0
Devices Equal Across Nodes|True
Memory Total                |24.000 GB
Memory Used                 |2.197 KB
Memory Used%                |0.0 %
Memory Avail                |24.000 GB
Memory Avail%               |100.0 %
License Usage Latest        |618.000 B
Namespaces Active           |1
Namespaces Total            |2
Active Features             |KVS,Batch
Number of rows: 17
~~~~~~~~~~~~~~~~~~~~~~~~~~~~~~~Namespace Summary~~~~~~~~~~~~~~~~~~~~~~~~~~~~~~~
Namespace|~~~~Drives~~~~|~~~~~~~~~Memory~~~~~~~~~|Replication|  Master|~License~
         |Total|Per-Node|   Total|Used%| Avail%|  Factors| Objects|~~Usage~~
         |     |        |        |     |       |         |        |  Latest
  bar    |   0 |       0|12.000 GB|0.0 %|100.0 %|       2|   0.000|  0.000 B
  test   |   0 |       0|12.000 GB|0.0 %|100.0 %|       2|  13.000|618.000 B
Number of rows: 2
```

Modifications

Using the `asadm` shell, you can modify the entire cluster dynamically. This can be dangerous as it affects the entire cluster, so if you are unsure of the setting you're changing you may want to consider running this on a single node using `asinfo` or use `asadm` in single node mode by passing `--single-node`:

```
$ asadm --single-node
```

Once you're in the `asadm` interactive terminal there are two main ways of changing configuration parameters. You can either execute the `asinfo` command from this shell or use the manage commands in `asadm`.

There is a safety mechanism to prevent accidental changes while in `asadm`. You must first enter a privileged mode using the `enable` command. If you run a command inside the `asadm` shell that changes something without being in privileged mode, you will see an error. Similarly, if you use `asinfo` commands inside of `asadm`, `asadm` will always assume `asinfo` is trying to make changes. Instead of executing the `asinfo` command inside `asadm`, an error will be thrown if not in privileged mode. The error will look something like this:

```
Admin> asinfo -v 'get-config:context=service'
ERROR: User must be in privileged mode to issue "asinfo" commands.
Type "enable" to enter privileged mode.
Admin>
```

To get past this, you can execute the `enable` command.

```
Admin> enable
Admin+>
```

You can see the + marker next to your prompt that informs you that you can execute changes and the safety is off. To stop running with `enable` you need to execute `disable`, or exit `asadm` and open a new session.

From this enabled `asadm` session, you can now execute `asinfo` commands and make changes. You can try making the same changes from the earlier `asinfo` example by changing the memory size:

```
Admin> sh config like memory-size
~test Namespace Configuration (2023-08-07 00:27:17 UTC)~
Memory-size|2147483648
Admin> enable
Admin+> asinfo -v 'set-config:context=namespace;id=test;memory-size=3G'
1.0.0.127.in-addr.arpa:3000 (1.2.3.4) returned:
ok
```

In a multinode cluster, you would see a response from each server. You can press the up arrow on your keyboard to get back to the show command and verify our changes made it to all servers:

```
Admin+> sh config like memory-size
~test Namespace Configuration (2023-08-07 00:28:53 UTC)~
Node |1.0.0.127.in-addr.arpa:3000
memory-size|3221225472
```

You can also make this change using the manage command in asadm. You can execute help manage config, which leads us naturally to help manage config namespace, as you will be changing the configuration parameter from the namespace context. This should show the following usage:

```
Usage: namespace <ns> [<subcontext>] param <parameter> to <value>
```

You can fill in the command with your real values and try it:

```
Admin+> manage config namespace test param memory-size to 2G
~Set Namespace Param memory-size to 2G~
Node|Response
1.0.0.127.in-addr.arpa:3000|ok
Number of rows: 1
Admin+>
```

Managing Index, ACL, UDF

Aerospike Enterprise Edition supports security features that allow fine-grained or broad basic controls on user ACLs through the manage acl command, the creation of secondary indexes on your data using the manage sindex command, and the registration of custom UDFs using manage udfs. UDFs are for very niche uses and are outside the scope of this book.

Aerospike Quick Look

As mentioned in Chapter 2, the Aerospike Quick Look (AQL) utility is a tool for interacting with some of the data in the Aerospike cluster. Using AQL you can read, write, and query data. This can be a big time saver if you want to check if a record exists or maybe inspect the bins of a specific record.

AQL does not have full feature parity with client drivers, so you may need to use an IDE to get full visibility into your data. AQL is unable to display data such as arbitrarily serialized bytes or protobuffed blobs.

Aside from reading and writing single keys, the most useful thing in AQL from an operator's perspective might be that you can look at the metadata of a key or find which node is the primary and secondary for that record. Let's get into the AQL interactive shell and explore some of this.

Unlike `asadm`, the `--help` menu does show us the commands you can run inside AQL:

```
$ aql --help
```

To get to the help page for connecting and entering the `aql` shell, you execute with `-?` on the end of the command:

```
$ aql -?
```

Some specific commands let you inspect the metadata and the source of a record. You will need a test record to inspect, so let's create that in AQL. Let's copy-paste the example from the help menu:

```
aql> INSERT INTO test.demo (PK, foo, bar, baz) VALUES ('key1', 123, 'abc', true)
```

This command has created one record in the demo set of the **test** namespace. Its PK is key1, and it has three bins: foo, bar, and baz, which have the values 123, abc, and true, respectively.

You can retrieve and display this record now:

```
aql> select * from test.demo where pk = "key1"
+--------+-----+-------+------+
| PK     | foo | bar   | baz  |
+--------+-----+-------+------+
| "key1" | 123 | "abc" | true |
+--------+-----+-------+------+
1 row in set (0.001 secs)
OK
```

 With some data types and especially very lengthy strings, AQL is unable to display all or in some cases any of the data in the chosen output type. Try using the RAW output type in those scenarios by typing SET OUTPUT RAW. You can view the other options on the help page or by executing help SET in the AQL session.

You can see your record exists and you get a nice table showing you what's in the record. As an administrator responsible for troubleshooting, you might also want to inspect the metadata:

```
aql> SET RECORD_PRINT_METADATA true
RECORD_PRINT_METADATA = true
aql> select * from test.demo where pk = "key1"
+--------+-----+-------+------+---------+-------+
| PK     | foo | bar   | baz  | {ttl}   | {gen} |
+--------+-----+-------+------+---------+-------+
| "key1" | 123 | "abc" | true | 2591764 | 1     |
+--------+-----+-------+------+---------+-------+
1 row in set (0.001 secs)
OK
```

You can change the setting to show metadata in AQL and run the select command again. This time, you can see TTL, representing the seconds until the record expires, and gen, representing the generation of the record.

asbackup and asrestore

The Aerospike tools package also contains utilities to make and restore backups. The backup utility works by performing a full namespace scan, and for each record it finds, it generates files that can be saved to a filesystem, another machine, or cloud storage. The restore utility reads in that data stored by asbackup, and for each record that it can construct, it performs a client write.

These utilities aren't doing block-level snapshots, write-ahead logs, or any advanced techniques. These are the same kinds of calls and interactions you can perform from the client driver (scan, read, write).

asbackup uses a scan to retrieve the data, reading records like a client and storing them where you specify. This behavior can be problematic, as you may have to worry about the data changing as you scan it in. Because there is no namespace-level or set-level locking, it's possible for some records to be taken in a backup from 10:00 a.m., while others aren't backed up until 11:00 am. If there is some relationship between these records, that could be problematic. The only locking mechanism during an asbackup is that the records are briefly locked while the read occurs to ensure consistency of a record.

At the same time, this behavior can be beneficial as it means you don't need to pause all client traffic while the database backup takes place.

The asbackup and asrestore commands each have their own help pages. Let's look at how you can back up and restore using default options:

```
$ asbackup -n test -o testfile
...
2023-08-13 18:39:37 UTC [INF] [29199] Backed up 84765 record(s), 0 secondary
index(es), 0 UDF file(s), 8037390 byte(s) in total (~94 B/rec)
$ ls -lhd testfile
-rw-r--r--@ 1 albert nosql 7.7M Jul 23 20:25 testfile
```

The asbackup command requires at a minimum a namespace (-n test) and somewhere to output the data (-o testfile). The asrestore command requires even less, as the backup file has metadata on which namespace the file should be written to.

Then to restore, you just feed the file in as input:

```
$ asrestore -i testfile
...
2023-08-13 18:40:49 UTC [INF] [30088] Opened backup file testfile
2023-08-13 18:40:49 UTC [INF] [30088] Restoring records
...
2023-08-13 18:41:02 UTC [INF] [30142] 0 UDF file(s), 0 secondary index(es),
84765 record(s) (145644 rec/s, 13486 KiB/s, 94 B/rec, retries: 0)
2023-08-13 18:41:02 UTC [INF] [30142] Expired 0 : skipped 0 : err_ignored 0 :
inserted 0: failed 84765 (existed 0 , fresher 84765)
2023-08-13 18:41:02 UTC [INF] [30142] 100% complete, ~0s remaining
$ echo $?
0
```

 The asrestore utility cannot restore the original generation of a record. If a record is created on the server that exists in the backup file, one of those versions will be clobbered. There is no merge strategy for records' bins, though the asrestore write is an upsert. You may want to consider passing the --unique parameter described in the help page to mean, "Skip records that already exist in the namespace; Don't touch them." Or you could use the --replace option, which does the opposite. If you inspect the output of this command, you can see that all records *successfully failed* to be restored as the command wasn't modified to clobber the existing data in the namespace, which may be valuable to us.

You can also stream this backup data over the network, write to a mounted filesystem, or even write directly to an s3 path by leveraging the stdout flags on asbackup output or asrestore output:

```
$ asbackup -o - | <do something with streaming stdout>
```

This can be helpful when streaming to proprietary storage solutions or compression software, like zstd:

```
$ asbackup -o - | pzstd -9 | cat > mybackup.zst
```

Similarly, asrestore's -i - reads from stdout:

```
$ do something | asrestore -i -
```

Or, continuing the example of restoring a compressed backup file:

```
$ cat mybackup.zst | pzstd -d | asrestore -i -
```

This makes `asrestore` and `asbackup` great tools you can use within the Linux GNU ecosystem of utilities. Aerospike recently added compression as a built-in feature under the `-z` flag, so this example isn't very relevant today. Still, it is good to illustrate some of the ways you can pair it with GNU utilities.

An additional notable feature of `asbackup` is the ability to perform incremental backups using `--modified-after` or `--modified-before`. Instead of performing a full backup each time, you can perform one full backup. Then take a backup of the things that have changed since the last backup. In the event of a restore you will restore the full backup and then each incremental backup in the order they were made. This greatly reduces the time to take backups of the database at the expense of complexity at restore time. It will become more complex the longer you go between taking a full backup.

asloglatency and asbench

The `asinfo` and `asadm` tools already show you some percentage distribution in various histogram buckets for latencies, but there is a more advanced utility called `asloglatency`. `asloglatency` is a Python utility for interpreting the histograms written in the Aerospike log file. This utility can be helpful for histograms not reported by the other tools, inspecting historically logged histograms, or if you want to inspect at a higher granularity on the fly. `asloglatency` allows you to inspect specific histograms and is particularly helpful if you need to enable and inspect microbenchmarks. Microbenchmarks allow a finer grain of visibility and latency tracking by adding additional histograms to aid in investigating where a problem may be.

For example, if you have read latency on your test namespace and are unsure what the cause is, you might want to enable read benchmarks to get extra logging on it:

```
$ asinfo -v 'set-config:context=namespace;id=test;enable-benchmarks-read=true'
```

 Microbenchmarks can add additional latency and greatly increase the amount of logging generated. You should always test in a nonproduction system, limit enabling this to one node at a time if possible, and remember to turn it off when troubleshooting is done.

This generates extra histograms in your log file, so let's find it in the log:

```
$ docker logs aerospike | grep hist | grep read
Aug 13 2023 19:14:42 GMT: INFO (info): (hist.c:320) histogram dump: {test}-read
(753 total) msec
Aug 13 2023 19:14:42 GMT: INFO (info): (hist.c:320) histogram dump: {test}-read-
start (753 total) msec
...
```

If you are using Docker, you need to export these logs to a file that `asloglatency` can interpret. You can skip this step if you already have your logs in a file:

```
$ docker logs aerospike > histogram.logs
$ grep "hist.c" histogram.logs | tail
Aug 13 2023 19:15:32 GMT: INFO (info): (hist.c:320) histogram dump: {test}-read-
local (753 total) msec
Aug 13 2023 19:15:32 GMT: INFO (info): (hist.c:331) (00: 0000000724) (01:
0000000006) (02: 0000000015) (03: 0000000007)
...
```

`hist.c` is responsible for logging the histograms, which is why you may want to use grep to search for that string in particular. You can see various histograms named on the line with histogram dump. The first line shows you the `test` namespace produced a `read-local` histogram. Now that you know where your logfile is, you can run `asloglatency` against it.

Let's first look at the main histogram for reads that is enabled by default:

```
$ asloglatency -l histogram.logs -h "{test}-read" -f head
```

And then you can drill into a specific slice of that read histogram, since you enabled these microbenchmarks:

```
$ asloglatency -l histogram.logs -h "{test}-read-local" -f head
Histogram Name : {test}-read-local
Log : histogram.logs
Aug 13 2023 19:07:01
%> (ms)
slice-to (sec)       1       8      64    ops/sec
-------------- ------ ------ ------ ----------
   19:20:12      10    0.00    0.00    0.00        0.0
   19:20:22      10    1.88    0.87    0.00       69.1
   19:20:32      10    0.59    0.00    0.00       67.9
   19:20:42      10    0.95    0.00    0.00       63.3
   19:20:52      10    0.47    0.00    0.00       64.4
   19:21:02      10    0.48    0.00    0.00       62.3
   19:21:12      10    0.48    0.00    0.00       63.0
   19:21:22      10    1.01    0.00    0.00       59.3
   19:21:32      10    0.83    0.00    0.00       59.9
   19:21:42      10    1.25    0.00    0.00       16.0
-------------- ------ ------ ------ ----------
          avg          0.16    0.05    0.00        6.7
          max          5.88    3.43    0.00       69.1
```

Inspecting this histogram, on the first line, you can see that between 19:20:12 and 19:20:22 0.87% of read local operations for the `test` namespace took more than 8 ms. Looking at the rest of the data, you can see that most of the time within this histogram, less than 2% of your operations exceed 1 ms, meaning 98% of your read-local operations are occurring in less than 1 ms.

If that's not enough resolution, you can add -e and -n to your command to change the number (-n) and exponential difference (-e) of the histogram buckets shown. For example, if you want a lot of granularity, you may choose to print 10 buckets (-n 10), each one exponent apart (-e 1):

```
$ asloglatency -l histogram.logs -h "{test}-read-local" -f head -e 1 -n 10
```

asloglatency works with all histograms found in the Aerospike logfile.

Throughout this chapter you've inspected latencies on a running container, but you never had to write an application to generate a workload. For various reasons like testing new hardware, testing capacity planning theories, or even testing disaster scenarios you may need a way to generate a workload synthetically. asbench is part of the Aerospike tools package and enables you to do that. There is an extensive number of options for customizing the workload to simulate the behavior you want, but to keep it short for the purposes of this chapter, here is the command to generate the preceding histograms:

```
$ asbench -n test -o 'B1000000' -w RU,50 -k 100 -t 120
```

This asbench command targets localhost by default, as many of the tools do. The specified namespace is test and you're using an object (record) specification for a 1,000,000-byte binary blob bin. The workload is 50% reads and 50% updates. The number of keys used in this run is limited to only 100 records. Finally, the asbench run is limited to 120 seconds of runtime.

When you run it, you'll first see the various workload stages and parameters, and then a ticker showing how many reads, writes, and failures asbench has generated:

```
$ asbench -n test -o 'B1000000' -w RU,50 -k 100 -t 10
...
namespace: test
set: testset
start-key: 1
keys/records: 100
...
2023-08-13 13:32:59.944 INFO write(tps=60 (hit=60 miss=0) timeouts=0 errors=0)
read(tps=83 (hit=83 miss=0) timeouts=0 errors=0) total(tps=143 (hit=143 miss=0)
timeouts=0 errors=0)
```

You can use this tool to synthetically run a benchmark against a running cluster, with a workload that matches your own. This should help characterize how Aerospike and your hardware handle the workload.

Security

Aerospike has various security features that enable you to run your cluster in a responsible and compliant way:

- TLS (*https://oreil.ly/Z8MlK*) to encrypt communication over the network from client to server or between servers
- ACLs to control specific users' access and quotas to specific namespaces and sets
- Aerospike Secret Agent, for secret retrieval of feature key and cert files
- Lightweight Directory Access Protocol (LDAP) to manage authentication to the servers
- Encryption-at-rest to ensure data flushed to storage devices is encrypted
- FIPS 140-2 certification, a specialized certification that meets US federal government requirements

All of these security features are behind an Aerospike Enterprise Edition server license, so if these are features you need, you can engage with the support staff to assist with any setup trouble. The public documentation available on Aerospike's website under the security overview section (*https://oreil.ly/p0occ*) should contain all the information you need to set this up. As you must have an Enterprise license to set these listed security features up, you can work with Enterprise support to help with concerns and setup help, so we won't go in depth on each of these features.

Summary

In this chapter we discussed the configuration file format and the importance of the configuration reference in setup and in daily operations work. You learned about the various tools that ship with Aerospike—`asinfo`, `asadm`, `aql`, `asbackup`, `asrestore`, `asloglatency`, and `asbench`—and how they are used for daily work, troubleshooting, and benchmarking. Finally, we gave a very brief overview of the security features that Aerospike offers in the Aerospike Enterprise Edition. In Chapter 8, we will build on that by discussing how you can use these utilities to perform upgrades and monitor the health of your cluster.

Monitoring and Best Practices

With every production system, you need to be able to quickly identify and respond to issues. You must ensure that you monitor Aerospike to keep your applications running smoothly in case of hardware issues, software bugs, configuration problems, and networking issues. This chapter will focus on guiding you toward a monitoring solution, discuss vital metrics to monitor, and review how to best respond to some problem scenarios. By the end of this chapter, you should have a grasp on how to monitor your Aerospike deployment, how to upgrade your servers running Aerospike, and some first steps to respond to operational demands.

Monitoring

There are two sides to monitoring Aerospike, from the client application using it and from Aerospike itself. Both are important for a robust and complete monitoring solution. If you monitor only the Aerospike database and the metrics it reports, you won't know if an operation fails to reach the server entirely. Similarly, if you only monitor the client application, you may miss out on critical information from the cluster itself or warning systems ramping up to an incident, such as lack of storage space.

Application Metrics

Within your Aerospike client application, you'll want to add monitoring around the latency of your calls and success rate, and you'll want to subscribe to the Aerospike logging interface. The latency and success rate measurements are up to you to implement by adding stopwatch timers, catching and counting exceptions and return codes. You can implement latency tracking by observing the clock before and after an operation like so:

```
Key key = new Key("test", "item", 1);
long startTime = System.nanoTime();
client.put(null, key, new Bin("name", "Stylish Couch"),
        new Bin("cost", 50000), new Bin("discount", 0.21));
long latency = System.nanoTime() - startTime;
System.out.printf("it took %d nanoseconds, %.02f milliseconds,
to write the data!\n", latency, (latency / 1_000_000.0));
```

This code produced the output:

```
it took 10065952 nanoseconds, 10.07 milliseconds, to write the data!
```

A more obscure, frequently overlooked, built-in feature is the client logging interface. You should implement the log callback function to log information from the client. Most entries are related to node membership, reachability, and cluster events. You can read about the logging interface and implementation on the Aerospike documentation website (*https://oreil.ly/5K7Pe*). You can enable the logging interface to stdout by adding just a line of code to set the callback:

```
Log.setCallbackStandard()
```

This allows the client driver to produce logs about cluster connectivity and membership. In this example, you will add a node to your Docker cluster, which is not reachable:

```
INFO -> Add node BB9020011AC4202 127.0.0.1 3100
it took 10065952 nanoseconds, 10.07 milliseconds, to write the data!
INFO -> Namespace test replication factor changed from 1 to 2
WARN -> Add node 172.17.0.3 3101 failed:
Error -8: java.net.SocketTimeoutException: Connect timed out
```

This can be an instrumental component in diagnosing issues, especially more difficult ones like intermittent partial network connectivity.

Aerospike Database Metrics

The Aerospike database produces a variety of metrics. There are metrics you'd expect from a database like space remaining, latency, and hit ratio, as well as deep forensic metrics you can review using Aerospike tools like `asloglatency`. You will want a system that collects these metrics to inform you if there is an issue, but you also want a system that will allow you to view trends in the data. Alerting can tell you if there is a given issue at a particular instant, and the trending allows you to determine if this is organic growth, related to a deployment, or some other event. Trends also allow you to evaluate if a particular threshold would be appropriate, given the history and recent changes in data, or if that threshold would be too noisy.

The Aerospike monitoring page (*https://oreil.ly/kYAkq*) lists common monitoring options and whether or not they support alerting and trending, which we summarize in Table 8-1.

Table 8-1. Monitoring options

Tool	Documentation	Alerting	Trending
Aerospike Monitoring Stack with Prometheus Exporter	Aerospike Monitoring Stack	Yes	Yes
Aerospike Management Console	Aerospike Management Console	Yes	No
ASADM	ASADM	No	No
Aerospike Logs	Aerospike Logs	No	Yes
Collectd	aerospike-community/aerospike-collectd	Yes[a]	Yes[a]
Graphite	aerospike-community/aerospike-graphite	No[a]	Yes
Nagios	aerospike-community/aerospike-nagios	Yes	No[a]
Zabbix	aerospike-community/aerospike-zabbix	Yes	Yes
Datadog	Datadog Docs	Yes	Yes
InfluxData	Telegraf Plugin for Aerospike	Yes	Yes

[a] Solution has third-party plug-in for alerting or trending

Among these various solutions for monitoring Aerospike, a common choice is Prometheus, which will be discussed in the remainder of the chapter. The thresholds, ideas, and methods apply to other solutions but the implementation will vary. For example, you could instead choose to use Nagios for alerting, paired with Graphite for trending and dashboard.

Prometheus

Prometheus is a monitoring platform that collects metrics from various servers into a local time-series database and can be set up with rules to aggregate and alert on these metrics. It is usually deployed as its own dedicated system and has rules set up to tell it where to find metrics and what to do with those metrics. You usually will have an alerting system integrated with it, and maybe a dashboarding utility like Grafana. An example topography may look something like Figure 8-1.

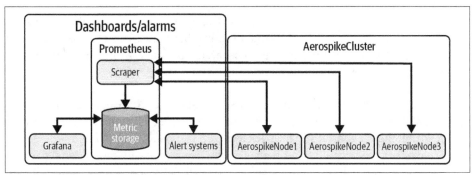

Figure 8-1. Prometheus monitoring topology example

Prometheus web requests

As part of its core functionality, Prometheus has a list of web addresses it needs to read. It performs a web request, GET, to each of the defined addresses and stores the metrics returned into a database. On some schedule, there is an internal system that performs queries based on rules from this data to generate alerts. The data stored in the system can also be graphed using Prometheus or a dashboarding utility like Grafana.

As Prometheus must poll every individual instance of Aerospike, you must configure each node to handle those requests. The requests Prometheus sends are web requests, which Aerospike doesn't support natively. The connecting glue that bridges the gap between an application and Prometheus is usually something called an *exporter*. The exporter runs alongside Aerospike to serve as a means of converting application-specific signals to Prometheus-style metrics and handles the web request.

You should be able to invoke web requests or use your browser, if the connectivity exists, to view the format of the web requests and the metrics present. Here is an example of a local exporter running to illustrate that you can simply curl the exporter's endpoint and read the result yourself:

```
$ curl -s http://localhost:9145/metrics
...
# HELP aerospike_node_up Aerospike node active status
# TYPE aerospike_node_up gauge
aerospike_node_up{build="6.4.0.10",cluster_name="null",
service="172.30.0.4:3000"} 1
...
```

This book will not cover the setup of Prometheus targets and service discovery implementations, as those will vary between organizations.

Aerospike exporter

The Aerospike exporter is typically installed as a systemd service along with the Aerospike database running on the same machine, but the exporter could also be run using Docker on the machine or even a separate container within the same pod if using a Kubernetes deployment.

Aerospike exporter service install.   If you wish to run the Aerospike exporter as a systemd-style service on a machine, you will need to be running Linux. The Aerospike Prometheus exporter binary packages (*https://oreil.ly/htTfw*) are on the download page under observability and management, where you can choose what package you need. Then you will install using the appropriate dpkg or rpm package installation command. In the example here, the ARM64 package will be installed on a Debian-like system using dpkg --install <file.deb> or dpkg -i <file.deb> for short:

```
# Download the 1.9.0 ARM64 Debian Aerospike Prometheus exporter package
wget https://download.aerospike.com/artifacts/aerospike-prometheus-exporter/
1.9.0/aerospike-prometheus-exporter_1.9.0_arm64.deb
# Install the package
dpkg -i aerospike-prometheus-exporter_1.9.0_arm64.deb
```

With the exporter package installed, you should also have a configuration file. This config file should have been created at */etc/aerospike-prometheus-exporter/ape.toml*. You should review this file to see what kind of customizations you can make and update it as needed, referring to the GitHub page (*https://oreil.ly/kUDs-*) for additional info. Some common changes to the exporter include blocklisting metrics to reduce the number of metrics Prometheus needs to ingest, adding a username and password for authentication, and customizing the port to connect to Aerospike or the port to listen on.

Now that the package is installed and you've added any necessary configuration changes to the file, you should be able to start the service using the `systemctl` command: `systemctl start aerospike-prometheus-exporter`. Once started, you can verify it remains running and read logging output using the command `systemctl status`:

```
$ sudo systemctl status aerospike-prometheus-exporter
• aerospike-prometheus-exporter.service - Aerospike Prometheus
...
Active: active (running) since Sat 2023-12-23 23:35:01 UTC; 2s ago
```

Once the exporter is up you should check that it is serving metrics and responding to web requests using a tool like `curl`:

```
$ curl -s http://localhost:9145/metrics
...
># HELP aerospike_node_ticks Counter that determines how many times the
Aerospike node was scraped for metrics.
# TYPE aerospike_node_ticks counter
aerospike_node_ticks 1
...
```

Aerospike exporter container.   Instead of running the binary, you can choose to run the Aerospike exporter container. The container can be leveraged as part of a container running inside a pod with a Kubernetes deployment, as part of a Docker Compose file, or ad hoc using a `docker run` command, which will be the fastest way to test it out. Aerospike publishes this container and provides various environmental variables to configure the exporter. (*https://oreil.ly/L034z*) If you run the Aerospike database as a local service and want to run the exporter in a container, the following command should work for you:

```
docker run --net=host --detach \
 -e AS_HOST=127.0.0.1 \
 -e AS_PORT=3000 \
 aerospike/aerospike-prometheus-exporter:1.14.0
```

This runs `aerospike-prometheus-exporter` container version 1.14.0 and passes environmental variables (`-e`) to connect to the Aerospike database running at IP 127.0.0.1 on port 3000. This command also specifies it should run on the host network, `--net=host`, which allows the Docker container to reach the host network instead of being stuck within the container itself. You also pass the `--detach` option, which allows Docker to run this in the background:

```
$ systemctl status aerospike
...
Active: active (running) since Sat 2023-12-23 23:46:58 UTC; 4min 56s ago
...
$ sudo docker ps
...
f74a059aaea1 aerospike/aerospike-prometheus-exporter:1.14.0
"/docker-entrypoint...." About a minute ago Up About a minute thirsty_morse
...
```

Again, you should test that it works by performing a web request against the exporter:

```
$ curl -s http://localhost:9145/metrics
...
aerospike_node_up{build="6.3.0.10",cluster_name="cakery",
service="10.0.2.15:3000"}
```

Metrics Reference

The Aerospike exporter relies on the same protocol available to Aerospike tools such as `asinfo` and `asadm`. The Aerospike database provides an `info` protocol, and when the exporter needs to fetch information from the database it will perform those same `info` calls and then reformat them as web requests. Since the metrics from all exporters originate from the Aerospike `info` protocol, you can use the metrics reference guide (*https://oreil.ly/BoSFM*) to help you find and understand their meaning.

With the Aerospike Prometheus exporter, the metrics are all prefixed with the name `aerospike_` followed by a metric *context* and finally the metric name and any specific labels. Picking a metric at random, the `aerospike_namespace_stor age_engine_stripe_free_wblocks` metric is a good specimen to evaluate:

```
$ curl -s http://localhost:9145/metrics
...
aerospike_namespace_storage_engine_stripe_free_wblocks{cluster_name="cakery",
ns="bar",service="10.0.2.15:3000",storage_engine="memory",
stripe="stripe-0.0xad002000",stripe_index="0"} 63
```

```
aerospike_namespace_storage_engine_stripe_free_wblocks
{cluster_name="cakery",
ns="test",service="10.0.2.15:3000",storage_engine="memory",
stripe="stripe-0.0xad001000",stripe_index="0"} 63
```

To look this metric up in the metric reference guide, you should be able to drop the aerospike_ prefix and search for storage_engine_stripe_free_wblocks inside of the namespace context. In reality, this exercise is less than exact and requires a little guesswork.

This particular metric is recorded in the metrics reference as storage-engine.device[ix].free_wblocks, which isn't the produced output! This is because of a compatibility change with some metrics—today Prometheus does not support metric names with brackets, dots, or even dashes. You will see this metric instead as aerospike_namespace_storage_engine_device_free_wblocks{device=ix} in Prometheus. You may find other metrics changed around some, but the information is typically moved into the labels section, the area inside the braces {...}, which is what happened with the device index [ix].

Along with the complexity added with the compatibility changes, you will also find some of the fields returned by the exporter are configuration parameters that are not found in the metrics guide. For example, a commonly tuned parameter in the configuration file is defrag_lwm_pct, which shows in our Prometheus metrics as aerospike_namespace_storage_engine_defrag_lwm_pct:

```
$ curl -s
http://localhost:9145/metrics|grep ^aerospike_namespace_storage_engine_
defrag_lwm_pct
aerospike_namespace_storage_engine_defrag_lwm_pct{cluster_name="cakery",
ns="bar",service="10.0.2.15:3000",storage_engine="memory"} 50
aerospike_namespace_storage_engine_defrag_lwm_pct{cluster_name="cakery",
ns="test",service="10.0.2.15:3000",storage_engine="memory"} 50
```

This metric reflects the configuration parameter defrag-lwm-pct, which you can look up using the configuration reference page. (*https://oreil.ly/Bt6Tm*) There is no straightforward way to identify whether the metrics are for runtime statistics or from configuration at query time; you will need to learn them or check both references.

Alert Rules and Dashboards

Now that you have Prometheus set up to scrape all your Aerospike servers' exporters, you need to create alert rules for Prometheus and dashboards. The folks at Aerospike have created a set of rules you may want to import from GitHub. (*https://oreil.ly/MNFXE*) These alert rules cover a wide variety of problems, so you should experiment with the queries and understand their meaning. At a minimum every deployment should be monitoring observability, which means the exporter is up and working, as well as latency and availability.

Alert rules

The first alert in the GitHub repo is a good example of the syntax for creating those alert rules. There is a distinct name for the alert rule, `AerospikeExporterAgentDown`, and some more information under an indent, showing that this all belongs to that rule:

```
- alert: AerospikeExporterAgentDown
  expr: up{job="aerospike"} == 0
  for: 30s
  labels:
  severity: warn
  annotations:
  summary: "Aerospike Prometheus exporter job {{ $labels.instance }} down"
  description: "{{ $labels.instance }} has been down for more than 30s."
```

The first line will be the expression `expr`—the query to run. This expression will evaluate to `True` if the exporter is not responding. Scenarios where this happens are usually related to hardware failure, Prometheus target misconfiguration, or complete failure of the exporter to start at all. If the expression evaluates to true for over `30s`, then it will trigger the alert to generate the text with the defined severity, which later can be consumed by some alerting or paging system.

 If this is the first time you've seen PromQL (Prometheus Query Language), it is best to first generate this data inside Prometheus where you can experiment with running queries while referencing the Prometheus basic query guide (*https://oreil.ly/lCFjJ*).

The next entry is also a vital one, detecting the condition where the Aerospike exporter is online, but the Aerospike database is offline or not responding. For brevity, the remaining snippets will be shortened to just the expression:

```
expr: aerospike_node_up{job="aerospike"} == 0
```

Scenarios where Aerospike is down but the exporter is not are usually caused by hardware issues, exporter misconfiguration such as not being able to authenticate to the cluster, or out-of-memory (OOM) events. Review the Aerospike server logs and system logs to determine the cause.

The next vital alerting rule you should monitor is that cluster integrity is `True(1)`:

```
expr: aerospike_node_stats_cluster_integrity == 0
```

This could be `0` because the node is unable to communicate with all nodes in the cluster, or perhaps the cluster rejects the node's request to join for some reason such as time drift exceeding a threshold. You can review the Aerospike logs for reasons why this might be false and may need to read the logs of the other nodes in the cluster to find the full picture as to why this may be.

Finally, the last table-stakes alert rule to mention is latency. You need to ensure that every node in the cluster is responding within an appropriate time frame:

```
expr: histogram_quantile(0.99,
(aerospike_latencies_read_ms_bucket{job="aerospike" })) > 4
```

This expression will be true, and fire, if the 99th percentile latency exceeds 4 ms for reads. There is a similar one for writes and you should customize this to fit your needs. This will fire if any particular *instance* has any namespace exceeding 4 ms. You can adjust this by adding a *sum* to aggregate across labels if, for example, you wanted to only know that the entire cluster's 99th percentile is achieving the desired result instead of every node being measured individually:

```
histogram_quantile(0.99, (sum by
(ns,le)(aerospike_latencies_read_ms_bucket{job="aerospike" })))
```

Dashboards

While you can create graphs and run queries on a Prometheus instance, you cannot create graphs across multiple Prometheus instances and multiple data sources, add custom visualizations, or save and share complex dashboards. Grafana is the tool usually paired with Prometheus for this purpose. Grafana can be connected to Prometheus, alongside other data sources, and then serve as the new frontend for running queries and dashboards. The Aerospike monitoring repository contains dashboards (*https://oreil.ly/vRwOe*) that can be imported and customized. By importing these dashboards, you'll be able to track these metrics and correlate events together more easily. You'll be up and running faster with less work required to build these gauges and graphs and present these indicators.

This should get you started with monitoring the health of existing clusters. Next, let's discuss the challenges and procedures for maintaining a current Aerospike version over time.

Software Updates

You must apply security and bug fix patches to the system on some cadence, for stability and security reasons. Aerospike posts release notes on their website (*https://oreil.ly/bGY9K*), which you should read if you think you may be encountering a bug that may already be fixed or want to understand the changes in the newer version. The major version changes sometimes come with special upgrade requirements and procedures that you need to read and understand, such as dropping a certain feature or a requirement to sanitize your storage devices after taking the daemon down. From version 6.3, the Aerospike vendor will support and backport hotfixes for released versions for up to two years after the release.

You should understand the mechanical steps of a typical upgrade. The upgrade steps can vary depending on if you are using the Community Edition or Aerospike Enterprise Edition, if you allow downtime, or if you have rack-awareness support, special upgrade requirements, or a special storage medium type. Reviewing various scenarios seems the most appropriate way to get started, and the first one you should know is the single rolling server restart.

Preparation

Suppose you have a 3-node cluster, with a replication factor of 2. If you need to upgrade this cluster, you must remove 1 node from the pool, which may drop your ability to handle requests by 33% (⅓). With larger clusters, this number becomes smaller and less impactful, but you must plan for it and understand the implications of removing a server from the cluster. Mainly, you need to make sure the other two instances in the server will be able to cope with the full load of requests and the replicated data size. A good rule of thumb is to apply this ratio to your various bottlenecks to determine ahead of time if you'll run into an issue:

```
((n-servers being removed + total-cluster-size) / total-cluster-size) *
bottleneck%
```

For example, say storage device space was your primary concern. If you have a 3-node cluster, with 34% storage space used, and need to remove 1 node, you should be able to forecast that easily as Aerospike balances things mostly linearly, especially with the `prefer-uniform-balance` Aerospike Enterprise Edition feature:

```
((1 + 3) / 3 ) * 34 = 45.34%
```

With most deployments using the default `high-water-disk-pct` of 50%, 45.34% is considered nearly full! This may be cause for alarm, depending on your needs.

Finally, the mechanism of *migrations* will be kicking in to re-replicate and redistribute the data through the remaining two nodes, which adds extra load. The migration process is tunable though, so you can mitigate this by tuning migrations (*https://oreil.ly/a2OLF*) to act slower and even entirely stop the process. However, you must be aware that this can cause some partitions to have and maintain an extra copy of data for some time period. If the forecast and final storage space used is 45.34%, for example, migrations may cause the cluster to exceed this final number while syncing replicas, maybe bringing us all the way up to 47%, for example, depending on how many active partitions are in-flight.

Now that you have your capacity checked and under watch, make sure that your cluster is stable. You should not remove servers from the cluster while the cluster is already undergoing migrations. You can utilize `asinfo` command `cluster-stable`, which you can read more about in the `asinfo` command guide:

```
Admin+> asinfo -v 'cluster-stable:size=2'
book-aerospike-1.book_default:3000 (172.28.0.3) returned:
ERROR::cluster-not-specified-size
```

If the cluster size is not as specified, or migrations are ongoing, the cluster-stable command will inform you that things are not in a stable state. If migrations are ongoing, chances are there was a recent network interruption or node lost from the cluster and you should address that before proceeding.

Upgrade

With the preparation out of the way, and your capacity being kept in check, you can now begin the upgrade. First you should understand how to upgrade a typical installation on a cluster with replication, without Aerospike Enterprise Edition features:

1. Stop Aerospike on the target node: sudo systemctl stop aerospike.

2. Perform any kernel or other software upgrades: yum upgrade, apt upgrade, etc.

3. Install the new version of Aerospike using the appropriate OS-specific command: dpkg -i, rpm -i, ../asinstall, etc.

4. Reboot if required. If kernel patches have been applied, this is usually required.

5. Start Aerospike: sudo systemctl start aerospike.

6. Verify Aerospike has started, is healthy, and joined the cluster: sudo systemctl status aerospike; asinfo -v status; asadm -e "info";. You should verify the server appears in asadm with all the other servers, and that Cluster Integrity is True on all members if this is not monitored by your alerting system.

7. Wait for migrations to finish.

In a nutshell, that's the upgrade procedure. But, you should know about the pitfalls, how to avoid them, and how to utilize the Aerospike Enterprise Edition license to move faster. The major points of contention and improvement are around steps 1 and 5, stopping and starting Aerospike.

Starting out with step 1, this is not a graceful handoff. When you have traffic flowing through the cluster and suddenly remove a server from the cluster, it causes a brief moment of impact. This is the same as unplugging a machine at random, which Aerospike handles quite well, but it is not ideal. The immediate impact is that in-flight transactions to that instance fail, and for the next second or two the applications will still attempt to connect and time out until the cluster and the applications recognize the server is gone. If you had any namespace with a replication-factor of 1, this complicates the matter further. With the Aerospike Enterprise Edition comes the ability to quiesce a node, which provides a smooth handoff of data and traffic. This will be covered later.

Coming to step 5, you must be aware of potential *zombie records*. If you are using storage devices with persistence, there is a scenario where some records that have been deleted will be *resurrected* in a sense while the database rebuilds the index from the persistent device. This is because of the way Aerospike is optimized to write to the storage device, where a delete won't immediately cause an operation to occur to a disk and expunge the data. The immediate result of a delete operation is that Aerospike will remove the entry from the primary index, but only later will it clean up and expunge the persisted data in a slow sweeping process called defragmentation.

This problem of zombie records can be addressed in two ways. First, you could wipe the storage devices before reintroducing the instance into the cluster and allow re-replication. This way, no deleted records that should have been deleted can be reintroduced. Second, you could utilize the Aerospike Enterprise Edition feature called tombstoning or durable deletes. The durable delete feature will write tombstones when a delete operation is performed. A tombstone is a marker that indicates the record should have been deleted from a specified time. Tombstones are written to storage to prevent the records from being reintroduced, allowing you to durably delete, but it causes the server to incur an I/O operation, so there is overhead.

Finally, the other major ways you can improve this are through rack awareness and rapid rebalance. With larger deployments, you can enable an Aerospike Enterprise Edition feature called rack awareness, which allows you to group several systems into a single sort of failure zone or a kind of shard. The main guarantee of rack awareness is that the replica and master copy of a record cannot reside in the same rack. This allows you to upgrade clusters with more nodes faster, as you can take down much larger groups of servers at a time (such as 10 servers at once) without downtime or data loss.

Rapid rebalance is another Aerospike Enterprise Edition feature that allows faster syncing of data. This is mainly useful if you are reintroducing a fast restarted Aerospike instance using the warm restart feature or have restarted a server and are allowing it to read back from a storage device. As an instance comes back into the cluster carrying its own data, the cluster will perform comparisons on the data coming from that node to the current cluster's data. If there is a record that exists in the cluster already, and a record that exists on the node that was restarted, there must be a resolution as to which record to choose. Depending on the `conflict-resolution-policy` configuration specified, the cluster will choose either the existing or the incoming version of the record. With rapid rebalance, the cluster is able to do this in much larger batches and can bring migration time down from hours to minutes.

With migrations and this type of conflict resolution scenario, it should be noted that this is not a merge strategy. One version of the record will "win" and clobber the other version of the record. The two resolution methods are based on the generation counter or the last update time, usually preferring the newer version of the record. The cross-datacenter replication (XDR) feature has similar guarantees with conflict resolution. If this is inappropriate for your application, you should avoid this scenario by not introducing potentially stale data into the cluster.

Quiesce

Quiesce is an Aerospike Enterprise Edition feature that allows you to gracefully remove a server from the cluster. You can read the full detailed guide on quiescing on the Aerospike website (*https://oreil.ly/NiaBP*). When you quiesce a node, the cluster will immediately begin moving data off the node and the application transactions will follow where the data goes:

```
Admin+> manage quiesce with <Node to remove>
Admin+> manage recluster
Admin+> sh stat like quiesce
```

Once you quiesce a node, you need to allow the records and transactions to drain off of it. Depending on your replication and consistency requirements, this could take between a couple of minutes and a few hours. This allows smooth handoff of the data to another node and prevents putting your cluster in a risky state. As this is an Aerospike Enterprise Edition–only feature, this strategy is something you should discuss with your Enterprise contact.

Once you restart a node after it was quiesced and drained, it should come back online and join the cluster as a regular nonquiesced node and begin taking on load.

Troubleshooting

Something eventually will go wrong, and when it does you need to be ready. This section will guide you on some of the common places to look for issues and what the appropriate response may be. The Aerospike troubleshooting guide (*https://oreil.ly/IRlRg*) is a good resource. There is no one prescribed solution to any particular issue, but instead you should have the tools and information at your disposal to find where the issue is.

Chapter 7 covers how to configure and access logging. Usually, you'll be able to find your log at */var/log/aerospike/aerospike.log* or `journalctl -u aerospike`. The logfile should be your first stop for any issues related to clustering, cluster membership, or trying to understand the order of events in some problem. Along with the Aerospike logfile, you should be familiar with checking the health of the hardware and hardware logs. For physical machines this usually will be through a utility like `ipmitool` or `ras-mc-ctl`. For both physical and cloud machines, you should be able to find hardware-related logs by using the `dmesg` command and checking the kernel log.

Aside from looking at the logfile of the problematic node, for clustering- or membership-related issues you should also explicitly locate and review the logs of the *principal* node. Aerospike uses a special protocol for cluster membership, called Paxos. With Paxos there is always an elected leader for the cluster, which is referred to as the principal, whose additional job is to janitor and gate-keep cluster membership. It is important to be able to identify the principal node and to inspect it, as it will contain the logs and reasons for why membership was rejected.

The easiest method for identifying the principal node is using the `asadm` command `info network` and looking for the server listed in *green* with an asterisk next to it. Once on the principal node, consider looking at clustering-related messages, `journalctl -u aerospike |grep clustering|less`, or noninformational messages, `journalctl -u aerospike|grep -v INFO|less`.

With latency-related issues, or throughput bottlenecks, you'll need to consider a whole host of potential bottlenecks. This is where supplemental monitoring and homogeneity will help you. The *microbenchmarks* referenced in Chapter 7 will also help you pinpoint those bottlenecks.

Along with the Aerospike Prometheus exporter, you should consider running the *node* exporter. The node exporter will collect various statistics on server resources such as processor frequency, storage device latency, storage device queue depth, network throughput, and much more. For all these metrics, there are prebuilt and shared Grafana dashboards in the community to help graph and compare them.

Homogeneity across a cluster can provide invaluable insight into an issue and should not be undermined. If all the hardware in the cluster is the same, then all the latencies, CPU utilizations, storage device utilizations, etc., should also be nearly the same. This is because of the proficient way that Aerospike balances traffic horizontally. If you observe that in your cluster of ten nodes, for example, one node is performing the same work but struggling much more than the other nine nodes, it's likely you have some bad hardware there. Similarly, if you have a large deployment and see one *rack* struggling, you may be able to quickly identify a networking issue. This isn't a hard requirement of Aerospike but we strongly recommend you keep the cluster homogenous if at all possible for running long-term clusters.

The Aerospike community is also developing features to help operators troubleshoot and maintain their clusters more efficiently by embedding new commands inside the `asadm` utility. The `show best-practices` command will review the configuration of the cluster and display warnings if certain parameters are not within Aerospike's recommendations.

Finally, the most important recommendation is planning. Work with your developers and have regular meetings on new features and requirements, run tests to determine the limits of your hardware, and stay ahead on capacity requests. This will help you avoid running into trouble.

Summary

You've learned about Prometheus and its exporters, and how to use them to your advantage in comparing trends and monitoring live issues. You should understand now how to reference metric names in the guide and find what they mean and how to create alarms on them, especially latency, availability, and observability. You've learned how to upgrade Aerospike, along with pitfalls and ways to expedite the process. Common troubleshooting methods were also covered to ensure you are able to start pinpointing problems when they occur. In the next chapter, you'll learn about some of the more advanced aspects of Aerospike's functionality and architecture.

## CHAPTER 9

Advanced Concepts

Some of the most challenging use cases go beyond the basic idea of running consumer services from a single location. Geographically distributed deployments are often used for deploying real-time services that serve large numbers (millions to billions) of consumers. These services typically require predictable low-latency SLAs (in milliseconds) as well as round-the-clock availability to ensure a great real-time consumer experience. Essentially the goal is to provide the first customer and the billionth customer the same engaging user experience while also ensuring that the service is always available. Replication of data across geographically distributed sites is essential to improve availability of real-time mission-critical services, such as many financial systems, ecommerce sites, telco services, and ticket reservation systems.

Many production services require a distributed database to be set up across multiple sites for resiliency and availability. Such geodistribution can be done using synchronous or asynchronous replication.

Only by using synchronous replication can consistency between distributed system components be provided, which will restrict availability during partitioning. Additionally, a synchronous active-active system will create higher latencies in the normal situation for writes that can run into tens or even hundreds of milliseconds if sites are distributed across thousands of miles in cross-continent deployments.

Figure 9-1 is an example of a synchronous active-active deployment. Here, a single Aerospike cluster is distributed across three sites and three racks with each site having an entire copy of the database. Synchronous replication causes write latencies to be between 100 and 200 milliseconds while read latencies in normal operation can be very low (submillisecond). While the system can survive a single site failure with diminished read performance, more complex failures could make all or part of the system unavailable.

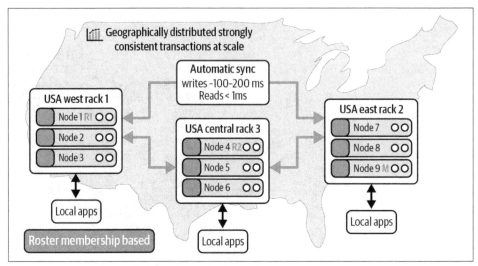

Figure 9-1. A multisite cluster that spans large distances

A good example use case that can use synchronous replication is the Banca d'Italia launch of Target Instant Payment Settlement (TIPS) (*https://oreil.ly/UD9ig*), which "guarantees settlement within seconds and is unique in doing this directly in central bank money." Consistency requirements are most stringent here and no one would use a payment system that occasionally loses their money, so not a single record can be lost in any case whatsoever.

However, most high-performance applications in the consumer space cannot tolerate the high write latencies required for synchronous replication nor the periodic lack of availability that results during split-brain conditions, when parts of the cluster can't communicate with other parts. In the example of Paypal's pipeline for fraud detection (*https://oreil.ly/QqukJ*) in their payment systems, machine learning and AI algorithms are used to generate a fraud score in real time (~100–200 ms). Typically, hundreds of reads are made to the database to generate the fraud score and dozens of writes are needed to store the recent history. The algorithms are only effective if recent behavioral data is input into the AI model for scoring. So, providing access to recently written transaction histories is imperative for preventing fraud before it happens, rather than detecting it after the fact. This means writes and reads with low latency are a prerequisite.

More examples of such use cases abound in the areas of risk management, recommendation engines, real-time bidding (RTB) for advertising, etc. In these use cases, it is important to process recent data efficiently, but a slightly relaxed consistency level is sufficient, unlike in the payment settlement case described earlier. As a result, relaxing consistency is acceptable for these kinds of applications to obtain extremely low read/write latencies, higher throughput, and very high availability. This means asynchronous replication is the best option for these applications.

Numerous synchronous and asynchronous replication strategies are widely used with the Aerospike database. At the time of writing this, the features referred to in this chapter are only available in the Aerospike Enterprise Edition.

Synchronous Active-Active System

Aerospike supports multisite clustering where a single cluster spans multiple geographies, as shown in Figure 9-1. This allows you to deploy shared databases across distant sites and cloud regions with no risk of data loss. Automated failovers, high resiliency, and strong performance are the foundation of Aerospike's implementation. Two features underpin Aerospike multisite clustering: rack awareness and strong consistency.

Rack awareness allows replicas of data partitions to be stored on different hardware failure groups (different racks). Administrators can configure each rack to store a full copy of all data through replication factor settings, maximizing data availability and local read performance. Aerospike evenly distributes data among all nodes within each rack.

Only one node on one rack maintains a master copy of a given data partition at any time. Other nodes (located on other racks) store replicas, which Aerospike automatically synchronizes with the master. As mentioned in detail in Chapter 5, Aerospike uses a roster (a list of nodes that are intended to be present) rather than a quorum to ensure the full data set is accessible. The roster combined with the partition map tracks the locations of masters and replicas. It also understands the racks and nodes of a healthy cluster.

In the configuration illustrated in Figure 9-1, each datacenter has one rack with three nodes, and each node has a copy of the roster. Given a replication factor of three, this example shows the roster-master copy of a data partition on Node 9 (Rack 2); replicas exist on Node 1 (Rack 1) and Node 4 (Rack 3).

You can configure Aerospike clients to route an application's request to read a data record from the local datacenter. In the deployment configuration shown in Figure 9-1, a full copy of the database exists on each rack (at each site in this case). Therefore, by intelligently processing read requests, Aerospike can deliver submillisecond read latencies in this cluster during normal operation.

Writes are processed differently. For consistency across the cluster, Aerospike routes each write to the node with the current master of the data. The master node ensures that the write is applied to its copy and all replicas before committing the operation. Routing writes and synchronizing replicas introduces overhead, so writes aren't as fast as reads. In the cross-continent configuration, latencies averaging between 100 and 200 milliseconds have been observed.

An Aerospike multisite cluster follows the same rules for enforcing strong data consistency as a single-site cluster (described in Chapter 5), automatically taking corrective actions for most common scenarios. For example, if the roster-master becomes unavailable due to a node or network failure, Aerospike designates a new master from the available replicas and creates new replicas as needed to satisfy the replication factor. In a multisite cluster, the new master will typically be on another rack.

Consider a scenario in which one site becomes unavailable, perhaps due to a network or power failure. Let's say that the USA East site (Rack 2) is unreachable by the rest of the cluster. Aerospike will automatically form a new subcluster consisting of USA West (Rack 1) and USA Central (Rack 3) to continue to service reads and writes without any operator intervention. In this degraded system, by applying the consistency rules as described in Chapter 5, all data will be made available with complete consistency in Racks 1 and 3, while no transactions (reads or writes) will be allowed in Rack 2. Note that when Rack 2 rejoins the cluster, the partitioning schemes, clustering algorithms, and strong consistency rules will ensure that the rejoining will be done smoothly with no operator intervention and eventually the cluster will return to steady state after accurately and safely merging in the changes that happened during the split-brain situation.

Note that there are split-brain situations where the system will just become either wholly or partially unavailable to preserve consistency (e.g., the case where all three sites in Figure 9-1 lose contact with each other simultaneously).

Asynchronous System

The Aerospike subsystem that implements asynchronous replication is called *XDR*. This was originally an acronym for *cross-datacenter replication*, but that name is not entirely accurate due to ubiquitous deployments on the cloud. From here on, we will simply use XDR to refer to the cross-cluster replication system independent of whether the clusters are in datacenters, cloud regions, cloud availability zones, etc.

There are three main use cases for the asynchronous replication architecture in Aerospike:

Disaster recovery
  This enables a consumer-oriented service, such as internet or mobile, to stay up during catastrophic failures.

Part of a content delivery network (CDN)
When Aerospike is used as part of a CDN, the consumer applications and their respective data need to be located close to the end user location to provide the best possible user experience.

Cluster duplication
When duplicating an existing cluster, asynchronous replication allows setting up a new cluster and transferring all data and workload from the existing cluster to the new one without any interruption in service.

Aerospike's asynchronous replication architecture uses the cluster as the basic unit for replication between geographically distributed sites. All replication between nodes of a single cluster is synchronous by default, and all replication between clusters is asynchronous as shown in Figure 9-2. The system supports two major kinds of topologies, active-passive and active-active.

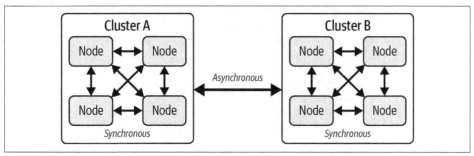

Figure 9-2. Replication between clusters is asynchronous

Active-Passive Topologies

A simple active-passive topology is shown in Figure 9-3. The active cluster, A, accepts application writes and sends these to the passive cluster, B, where it's applied locally. The active-passive behavior is indicated by the one-way arrows linking the clusters. There are no application writes directly written to cluster B. Applications can read from the passive cluster, but the latest data will not be available in the passive cluster until the writes to the active cluster have been received and applied to the passive database cluster B. The time it takes for a committed write in the active cluster to arrive at the passive cluster is called the *lag*.

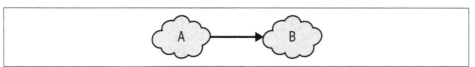

Figure 9-3. Simple active-passive

An active-passive topology that forwards the writes from one cluster to another by linking them in a linear chain is useful in some situations. In the case illustrated in Figure 9-4, application writes are sent to the active cluster, A. Cluster A ships its writes to passive cluster B, which in turn ships them to a second passive cluster C. The disadvantage of this scheme is that there is a cumulative delay in shipping data to clusters that are many hops from the active cluster.

Figure 9-4. Linear chained active-passive

Figure 9-5 illustrates a more complex active-passive topology. This topology, called a *star* topology, has one active cluster A that ships all its writes in parallel to the other clusters. A minimum of three clusters are required to create a star topology, one active cluster (A) and at least two passive clusters (e.g., D and E).

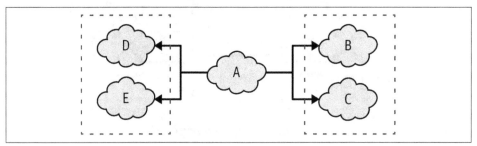

Figure 9-5. Complex active-passive (aka star topology); dotted lines indicate passive clusters

Active-Active Topologies

In an active-active setup, all clusters in the system can accept application writes and ship these to each other. A simple two-cluster active-active system is shown in Figure 9-6. In this case, there are two clusters, A and B. Both these clusters take writes from the application and ship their data writes to the other cluster.

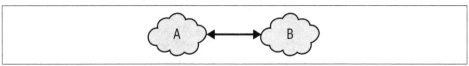

Figure 9-6. Simple active-active

If the same record is modified around the same time in both clusters, there is a potential for data conflicts to occur. There are strategies to design around this, such as convergence, which is covered later, but you need to be aware of this risk unique to XDR with active-active topologies.

In real-life situations, topologies can be very complex and include a mix of active-active and active-passive links. Figure 9-7 illustrates an example where there are four active clusters (A, B, C, and D). Each of these clusters is connected to the three other clusters with bidirectional links. This is called a *mesh* topology. Star and mesh topologies are the most used in complex real-world deployments.

Additionally, there is a link from the active cluster D to a passive cluster E. Each active cluster (A, B, C, and D) allows application writes, while the passive cluster E only gets changes from cluster D through the one-way replication link. Since D is connected to all other active clusters, E should eventually receive all the application data writes that occur at any of the active clusters.

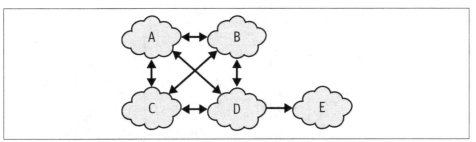

Figure 9-7. Complex active-active mesh topology plus an active-passive link

One thing to keep in mind is to avoid loops in the shipping configurations to ensure that the system does not get into an infinite loop by forwarding the same data changes repeatedly along the links that make the loop.

Shipping Strategy

Asynchronous replication uses the record metadata stored in the database indexes to determine the change list for shipping. The shipping algorithm in Aerospike is based on a combination of two key pieces of metadata: LUT and each partition's last ship time (LST). Aerospike keeps track of these in its index (typically memory resident). Any record in a partition whose LUT is greater than the partition's LST is a candidate for shipping. If the LUT of a record is more recent than the LST of the record's partition, the record will be shipped to remote clusters through the corresponding links that are active. Once shipping has completed the partition's LST is updated.

Aerospike supports the ability to ship subparts of changed records, such as a single bin, and implements a convergence feature that can resolve write conflicts in active-active topologies. This feature makes sure that the data is eventually the same in all the connected sites at the end of replication even if there are simultaneous updates to the same record in multiple sites. To achieve this, extra information about each bin's LUT is stored and used appropriately.

A typical setup of a globally distributed deployment with asynchronous replication is illustrated in Figure 9-8. As you can see there can be many globally distributed sites communicating to each other in complex topologies, supporting both active-active and active-passive deployments. The metadata used to track changes and the ability to ship subparts means that the asynchronous replication in Aerospike can be used in complex deployment topologies without concern about varying shipping speeds across multiple destinations with different network characteristics.

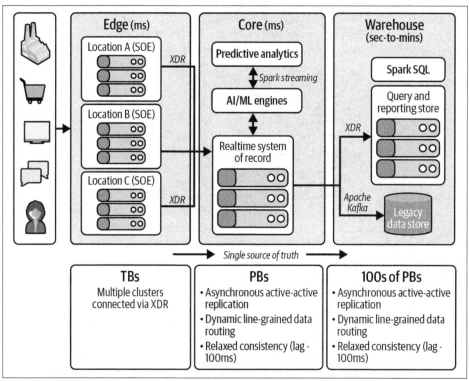

Figure 9-8. Global asynchronous replication using XDR

Rewind

One useful capability of XDR is that a database operator can specify a time in the past and request XDR to ship all the data that has changed since that time. This is called a rewind.

 Delete operations may not be shipped during a rewind as the database may not have that information stored in the database forever (any delete tombstones created are deleted periodically within the cluster once all the earlier copies of the data are removed). Outside of rewind operations, delete operations are typically forwarded to the remote clusters to keep them in sync.

The ability to rewind can be used to prepopulate new destination clusters from a source cluster using XDR. More commonly, the rewind is used to correct configuration mistakes that lead to missed records. It can also be used to work around any bugs in applications that resulted in some data not being properly updated in the source database and hence not replicated properly.

Convergence

When clusters are installed in complex topologies containing active-active and active-passive modes (Figure 9-7), concurrent updates to the same record can cause the values of the record in two destination clusters to differ when they are shipping the same data to each other. Aerospike implements a convergence scheme based on subparts of the record (bins) that have their LUT stored with them. With each bin the following data is tracked and shipped: LUT, cluster src-id, and the XDR write bit (a flag showing if that version of the bin is eligible to be shipped by XDR or not).

The convergence algorithm uses last writer wins (LWW) semantics. A bin value with a higher LUT can overwrite the bin value with lower LUT but not vice versa. If both LUTs match, the cluster src-id is used to break the tie, whichever is first in alphabetical order. This scheme assumes that the server's clocks are synchronized cluster-wide, but monotonically increasing clocks are good enough to result in good system behavior.

In Figure 9-9, you can see how Aerospike's algorithms implement convergence, aka strong eventual consistency. (The vertical axis represents time with the past at the top moving downward toward the future.) When there is no convergence, two clusters can both get updates, update 1 and 2. As they send them across to each other, the update written first can be put into the other cluster late, causing it to overwrite the second change, so cluster DC1 will have change 2, the correct data. Cluster DC1 sends update 1 late, so cluster DC2 has change 2 overwritten by change 1. It reverts to the incorrect data that was in the earlier change 1.

The right two clusters show what happens with the bin-convergence algorithms. Change 2 is written to DC1 after change 1, so it has the correct data. Change 1 arrives at cluster DC2, but the algorithms compare the last updated time and decide change 1 should not be applied. So, change 2 remains and both clusters have the correct data.

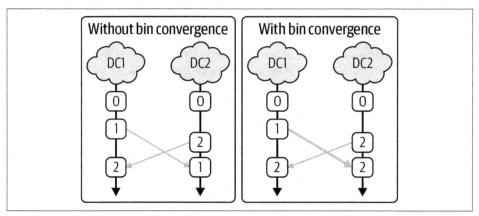

Figure 9-9. Bin convergence prevents out-of-order writes across clusters in different geos

Non-Aerospike Destinations

While the discussion has focused on Aerospike as the destination cluster so far, this replication strategy also works well with non-Aerospike destinations. There are a few key differences, however:

- For Aerospike destinations, XDR can autodiscover new nodes, detect node health, and provide partition-based routing.
- For non-Aerospike destinations, XDR can't autodiscover new nodes, can't auto-detect node health, and can support only digest-based load balancing.

So far, the assumption has been that network access from the source cluster to every node of the destination cluster is there and reliable. In the real world, there are many situations where that is not possible, especially for deployments that combine clusters deployed on multiple public clouds and private datacenters. For Aerospike destinations, a stateless *XDR proxy* can be placed behind a load balancer to translate the network protocols of the Aerospike cluster on the destination side, as in the bottom two topologies shown in Figure 9-10. For non-Aerospike destinations, there is an event stream processing (ESP) connector that can provide an HTTP interface to make it even easier to translate protocols of one type to another as in the bottom topology shown in Figure 9-10.

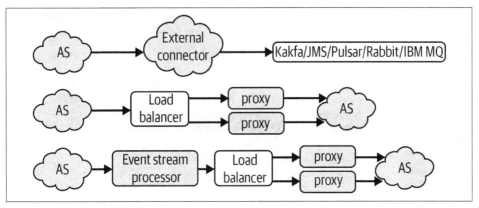

Figure 9-10. Proxying XDR requests

Ordering Limitations

Due to the asynchronous nature of the replication strategy, there are limitations for enforcing ordering of the updates across clusters that are in sites located geographically far apart. While the partition ID and digest affinities to nodes help in normal situations, there are exceptions in the case of timeouts, destination node failures (real or perceived), dynamic service thread changes, and source node failures (real or perceived). You can see an example of an out-of-order message delivery in Figure 9-11 that results in DC2 having the earlier value. This case assumes that bin convergence is not used to enforce ordering in DC2.

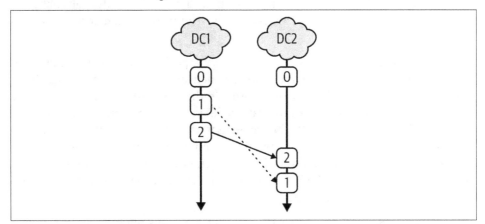

Figure 9-11. Out-of-order message delivery

The ability to enforce ordering natively in the asynchronous replication strategies is limited. You can improve the ordering limitations by introducing bin convergence. Since bin convergence is quite expensive, there are lightweight alternatives that are not perfect, but a major improvement over the default shipping algorithm. Typically, ordering is introduced between the source cluster and the destination cluster by using the XDR proxy or the ESP connector. Some of the pros and cons of these approaches are shown in Table 9-1.

Table 9-1. Ordering without bin convergence (AS/C = target Aerospike cluster, X = source cluster shipping through, XDR P = proxy, LB = load balancer, ESP = event stream processor)

	X → AS/C	X → P → AS/C	X → LB → P → AS/C	X → ESP → LB → P → AS/C
1: XDR timeouts	Problem	P helps	P can't help	ESP helps
2: P up/down	NA	P can't help	P can't help	ESP helps
4: Src up/down	Problem	P helps	P can't help	ESP can't help

Strong Consistency Can Be Fast

As introduced in Chapter 1, Aerospike is the obvious evidence that strong consistency can be fast. The basic concepts of many of the strategies that make this possible are in Chapter 5. Let's look at how they all work together and dive deeper into some of those strategies.

For horizontal scaling, Aerospike uses a shared-nothing architecture in which all nodes forming the database cluster are identical in terms of CPU, memory, storage, and networking capacity. A key component of this scheme is a uniform data partitioning algorithm that eliminates skew in terms of data distribution across database cluster nodes, thus ensuring there are no hotspots. Rack-aware deployments, dynamic data rebalancing, and a smart client with one hop to data all make the system extremely efficient and elastic even as the load increases and decreases in real time.

For vertical scaling, the database leverages every aspect of the hardware and cloud infrastructure (CPU, main memory, storage, network, etc.) to ensure that 100% of the system infrastructure is used to provide the best system performance. The HMA can enable storing of real-time data in SSDs. Since SSDs can be used to store up to 100 TB of data per node, this condenses cluster node counts but increases per-node transaction requirements by 10× or more. To support this, Aerospike is written in C language and employs advanced techniques like CPU pinning, NUMA pinning (*https://oreil.ly/zGWLL*), streamlining, network queueing, etc., to maximize processing efficiency on each node.

A key challenge to implementing strong consistency in a distributed system is finding a way to maintain high performance as well as a fair amount of availability. Because of Aerospike's horizontal and vertical scaling efficiencies, it can use a write-all, read-one synchronization scheme.

To improve availability during failures, the strong consistency algorithm is based on the list of cluster nodes called the roster. During node failures and/or network failures, the roster information is used to define rules for making decisions on when a particular data item is available. These rules ensure the availability of *all* data in the strongly consistent database system during common maintenance or failure situations:

- Two-way split-brain where the cluster splits into exactly two subclusters
- Rolling upgrade (needs a minimum of two copies in the cluster)
- A single site failure of a three-copy database system running on three racks across three sites

One key advantage of this scheme is that it can preserve strong consistency using two copies. This results in a highly efficient implementation of strong consistency, compared to other consensus-based schemes (e.g., Raft (*https://raft.github.io*)). Aerospike benchmark results of a 5-node cluster operating at different levels of consistency are shown in Table 9-2. These were run with 500 million keys, replication factor 2. Aerospike was configured for in-memory with persistence. Note that linearizability (*https://oreil.ly/ZtWd9*) and sequential consistency (*https://oreil.ly/QQW8T*) are two forms of strong consistency—i.e., there is no data loss possible in either of these settings. The measurements show virtually identical TPS (transactions per second) and read/write latencies in the sequential consistency (CP mode—prioritizing consistency) and relaxed consistency cases (AP mode—prioritizing availability). In this situation, Aerospike has virtually eliminated the performance gap between strong and relaxed consistency configurations.

Table 9-2. Performance comparison of various consistency settings

	Linearizability, no data loss, CP mode	Seq. consistency, no data loss, CP mode	Relaxed consistency, AP mode
TPS	1.87 million	5.95 million	6 million
Read	548 µs	225 µs	220 µs
Write	630 µs	640 µs	640 µs

Summary

In this chapter, you learned about synchronous and asynchronous replication strategies as well as a fast transactional implementation of strong consistency. The Aerospike database with these capabilities is typically used by real-time consumer applications that require high read and write throughput combined with a need to run in multiple sites that are far apart from each other. In Chapter 10, you'll see some use cases with these and other challenging requirements that Aerospike is well designed to fill.

## CHAPTER 10

Aerospike Practical Examples

By now you should have a good understanding of Aerospike. You have learned how to store data, query data, and the architecture behind it, which is designed for incredibly fast performance with the ability to scale to petabytes of data and tens of millions of transactions per second. In this chapter you will learn about some common use cases for Aerospike.

The use cases here are all real-world examples of where Aerospike shines. These typically involve the need for very fast access times, short SLAs, reasonably large data volumes, and high importance to the business. The use cases we will be covering are:

- User profile store
- Customer 360
- Fraud detection

User Profile Store

User profile stores contain information about users, typically related to a single use case. They typically contain current, historical, and derived data about a user. This information is used to enhance interactions with the customer, allowing real-time decisioning about products, interests, and so on.

One example of a user profile is in the advertising technology (ad-tech) vertical to store audience segmentation data on a per-user basis. Normally a user is identified by a cookie containing a unique ID. This ID can identify the user's device (phone, tablet, computer, etc.) and ad-tech companies will typically store information against this ID regarding websites that device has visited, purchases made on the device, and so on. This enables them to build up a picture of the interests the user of that device has.

Note that this is a simplistic view. Advanced ad-tech companies typically try to match users across devices, so if the same user uses a phone and tablet they see an aggregated view of their interests. Also, amalgamated views of interests across households are not uncommon. For example, consider a family in a household who owns a dog. One person in the household might typically shop for dog food, but it's not unlikely that other people in the household might also respond positively to seeing ads for dog food.

Recent changes in privacy regulations such as Europe's General Data Protection Regulation (GDPR) have seen a reduction in the dependency on cookies and device IDs. However, there are various other methods (*https://oreil.ly/SGTw7*) that ad-tech companies now rely on to be able to show more targeted ads to people such as probabilistic, synthetic IDs. These typically rely on more data, not less, exacerbating the need for user profile stores.

Audience segmentation for RTB is a special case of user profile stores. It's a form of personalization that happens tens of millions of times per second, as ads are served in real time around the world to people using apps, visiting web pages, and watching streaming content. It's simple to describe, and generally applicable to other forms of online personalization. The ad-tech companies enter a bidding process in an auction to display an ad on users' screens based on what companies have asked them to show ads and how likely they believe the user is to click on the ad. The more likely they feel the user will click on an ad that they have available, the more they can bid.

This is where the information about the users' interests comes into play. If an ad-tech knows a user is interested in football, for example, and has a merchant who has a sale on football jerseys, they will probably bid more for the right to show their ad to that user. However, this whole end-to-end auction happens in a literal blink of an eye—about a hundred milliseconds. That means the reading of the users' interests must be very, very fast. To leave room for processing and network transmission this must occur in no more than about 10 milliseconds, and the more information that can be loaded in that time, the better a determination can be made about what ad to show to the user.

It is also important that the segments a user has can expire. If someone has not viewed information on car batteries, for example, for more than a month, it's probably no longer relevant to them. Hence many ad-tech companies will expire audience segments after a period of time, typically 30 or 60 days.

Data Model

In this case there is an obvious PK, the user ID or cookie ID. All the user segments could be stored inside a list or map in a record associated with that key. However, the segments need to have an expiry TTL, which Aerospike supports only at the record level, which is not granular enough to be able to expire records inside a map in a record.

For the sake of this example, assume that the ad-tech is using user IDs instead of cookie IDs. One possible data model would be to store the PK as a compound key, with the user ID as the first part and a sequence number as the second part. So if the user ID is "1234" and there are three audience segments the PKs would be "1234:1," "1234:2," "1234:3," and so on. A representation of this might look like Figure 10-1.

PK	Expiry	Interest	Source
1234:1	1710581206635	FOOTBALL	footballsite.com
1234:2	1710581296456	CRICKET	cricketsite.com
1234:3	1710681210167	BASKETBALL	basketballsite.com

Figure 10-1. Possible user profile data model

Note that the expiry is in milliseconds since the Unix epoch of 1/1/1970, and there is typically other information associated with each segment like where this segment was seen (the "Source" in this example).

This model has the advantage of being simple and able to automatically expire the segments through Aerospike's TTL mechanism. It's flexible as it's easy to add new bins to the model and extend as business requirements change.

However, there are a number of drawbacks too. These include:

- It's not obvious how to work out how many segments there are. One user might have five segments and another user might have one hundred. If you know how many segments there are for a user a batch read can be used to pull in all the segments for that user. However, working out the number of segments would typically require an extra read, costing time.

  For example, consider the segments in Figure 10-1. There are initially three, but what if the "cricket" segment hasn't been seen for a while and has expired, and two new segments have been added? So the "active" segment IDs would be "1234:1," "1234:3," "1234:4," and "1234:5." Over time, it becomes increasingly hard to know which keys relate to segments that are active, and trying to read segments that have expired takes time, which is undesirable.

  A secondary index could be used for this purpose too, requiring the user ID in a separate bin. Then a secondary index query could be issued with `Fil ter.equal("userId", value)`; however, secondary index queries are not as fast as primary index queries and performance is critical in this use case.

- The records are typically small. Remember that each record in Aerospike requires 64 bytes of primary index storage. One large ad-tech who uses Aerospike for this use case has around 50 billion records. (Obviously, they're using cookie IDs rather than user IDs.) If there are on average a thousand segments per cookie, that's 50 *trillion* records. Multiply this by 64 bytes and they would require almost 3 petabytes of storage for their primary index, which is typically stored in RAM for performance reasons. That's a lot of RAM, and a lot of records Aerospike needs to scan to determine if they have expired or not!

Hence a better data model would be to use a single record per user with a PK of the user ID. The interests could be stored in a map with the segment ID as the map key and a list containing the record expiry and other information as the map value. This is shown in Figure 10-2.

PK	Segments

1234	{
	"FOOTBALL" : [1710581206635, "footballsite.com"],
	"CRICKET": [1710581296456, "cricketsite.com"],
	"BASKETBALL" : [1710681210167, "basketballsite.com"]
	}

Figure 10-2. Better user profile data model

Expiry of Elements

This design has many advantages over the first proposed design. These include:

- It uses only a single key-value read to get all of the segments for a single user, resulting in optimal performance.
- The number of records equals the number of users, so in the preceding example there would be 50 billion records, requiring about 3 TB of primary index storage across the cluster. While this sounds like a lot, it is important to note that this is a very large use case. Assume each segment and associated data is 50 bytes, and each user has on average a thousand segments. (This is a little higher than might be seen in production but this is for the sake of illustration). That means the amount of data to be stored in the database is: 50 bytes × 1000 segments × 50 billion records ~= 2.3 PB.

That's a lot of data! It would definitely need a large cluster size, and 3 TB spread across a cluster that large is not a large amount of RAM per node. Note that multiple petabytes of data like this is not an issue for Aerospike, and large clusters like this one might be between 100 and 200 nodes, with high data density per node.

The only drawback to this approach is that Aerospike's built-in record expiration mechanism cannot be used to expire segments as they're map elements instead of records. However, if you recall in Chapter 6, a mechanism to remove elements by time range was discussed. That technique is used extensively in user profile use cases to remove elements that have expired.

As a reminder, this technique relies on having the expiration timestamp as the first element in the list of values, similar to what is shown in Figure 10-2. Retrieval of all nonexpired elements relies on calling getByValueRange. For example:

```
Date now = new Date().getTime();
Record record = client.operate(writePolicy, key,
    MapOperation.getByValueRange("segments",
        Value.get(Arrays.asList(now)), Value.INFINITY,
        MapReturnType.KEY));
```

The parameters to the getByValueRange call are the bin name (segments), the start time (now, wrapped in a list as the values are lists and Aerospike needs to compare objects of the same type), the end time (INFINITY), and the information to be returned, in this case just the key (the segment name). If a segment is valid, the expiry time will be in the future and these parameters select these entries.

There are a couple of options for removing expired segments. The first is to remove obsolete segments when a new segment is added. As this incurs a write anyway, the cost is fairly low. The code to that looks like:

```
long now = new Date().getTime();
long expiryMs = now + MS_IN_30_DAYS; // Add 30 days
List<Object> data = Arrays.asList(expiryMs, "pi.com");
client.operate(writePolicy, key,
    MapOperation.removeByValueRange("segments",
        Value.get(Arrays.asList(0)),
        Value.get(Arrays.asList(now)),
        MapReturnType.NONE),
    MapOperation.put(MapPolicy.Default, "segments",
        Value.get("ELECTRONICS"), Value.get(data)));
```

Note the call to removeByValueRange as one of the operations in the list to remove the expired segments. For further information on this, please refer to Chapter 6 where this example was covered in more detail.

At the time of writing, there is a CPU cost to the removeByValueRange operation if the records were stored on SSD. (This is planned to no longer be the case as of version 7.) The reason was that maps stored on SSDs, even those created with a map order of KEY_VALUE_ORDERED, only persisted the data sorted by the key. The index used to access the values in value order was not persisted, meaning that the map had to be sorted each time Aerospike needed to access it in value order.

Version 7 will introduce the ability to persist these indexes. This requires extra space on the SSDs for storage of the indexes but removes the need for CPU cycles to perform this sort. The way to persist a map index is to use `MapOpera tion.create(String binName, MapOrder order, boolean persistIndex)`. Note that persisting the map index in this case will also lower the CPU cost of the `getByVa lueRange` call in the retrieval path.

Another approach to removing these expired elements (if you don't yet have version 7 of Aerospike) is to use a background query with an operation. This is very efficient as the operation runs in the background on each of the servers, without the need for the client to wait until it finishes. You can also specify a maximum throughput rate to ensure server-side resources are not heavily taxed by the operation. Code for this could look like:

```
Statement stmt = new Statement();
stmt.setNamespace(NAMESPACE_NAME);
stmt.setSetName(SET_NAME);
stmt.setRecordsPerSecond(1000);

ExecuteTask task = client.execute(null, stmt,
    MapOperation.removeByValueRange(
        BIN_NAME, Value.NULL,
        Value.get(Arrays.asList(now)), MapReturnType.NONE));
task.waitTillComplete();
```

Note that the `waitTillComplete` call will force this thread to suspend until the background scan returns and may not be needed in your use case. The rate of execution has been throttled in this example using the `setRecordsPerSecond` method and this limits execution to a thousand records per second per server, not across the cluster.

Customer 360

Customer 360 refers to the holistic view an organization has of its customers. Most organizations acquire customer data and sentiment from a variety of different sources such as:

- Direct conversations
- Reviews on websites
- Marketing outreaches
- Monitoring of web site traffic
- Support calls

Traditionally, many of the systems interacting with customers have their own view of the customer's data rather than bringing them into a single, unified view. Customer relationship management (CRM) systems attempt to create a broader view of the customer across these disparate systems, but they often fail to satisfy the requirements of all the stakeholders who need access to the customer data.

To serve customers better, a unified model across disparate data sources is needed. Aerospike, with its ability to store unstructured data with rapid updates and reads, is great at this. However, like all systems that combine data from multiple sources, care must be taken to ensure that the data is unified in a format that is easy to query.

Such a system can coalesce data about a customer including:

Activity
How many times has this person been contacted, and what have been the results each time?

Intent
What has this person been shopping for, and what have they purchased?

Satisfaction
Have they expressed sentiments about their experiences so far, or can the business infer sentiment from other signals?

Influence
Does this customer have a platform to recommend your product to others or dissuade them from buying?

Preferences
How does this person want to be contacted, and when?

Context
Are there in-the-moment circumstances (e.g., an open service ticket) that affect whether to make an offer or not?

Effective Customer 360 solutions need to use a single repository to look at stored data and real-time information, apply AI and machine learning, anticipate the customer's next action or interest, and serve customized, personalized experiences. They can also identify which users are key influencers in their social and work circles and target those users with offers to help drive adoption of services.

Data Model

The data model for a Customer 360 use case is not as cut-and-dried as it is for a user profile store and depends upon organizational objectives. Some considerations are:

- How large will a single customer record become? If it's too big, should it be separated into multiple objects that refer to one another? This is particularly prevalent if there is data that grows over time, like emails sent to the customer.

- What are the real-time requirements? Some parts of the model will rarely be read or updated whereas others will have a high frequency of reads and updates. Storing information with rapid changes or read requirements in the same record with a lot of rarely read or rarely changing data can cause performance issues as Aerospike always reads or writes the whole record off storage.

- What is the structure of the data? If parts of the data arrive in JSON format, for example, should it be stored as a string for efficiency or pushed into Aerospike lists and maps for easy manipulation?

- How will the data be ingested? Will it be streamed in from disparate sources using Apache Kafka, Amazon Kinesis, or similar technologies? Is there a need to transform the data ingested from these streams so that the format in the database is different to the format on the wire?

Often, a single customer is broken into multiple records to facilitate the preceding considerations. Parts that change rapidly or grow over time form their own separate records, referenced from the main record either directly or indirectly.

For example, consider a telecom provider that services regional areas where call reliability is poor. A user is driving and talking on their phone, then enters a region where signal quality is poor and the call drops. The Customer 360 view of that customer could well have a "sentiment rate," showing the level of satisfaction with the provider. This may be on the customer's main record. There are probably also call data records (CDRs) that show the user's call history and any issues the customer has experienced. A sample workflow might be similar to that shown in Figure 10-3.

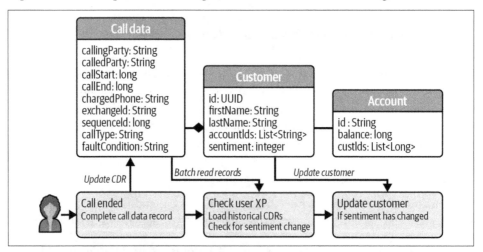

Figure 10-3. Telecom customer data update due to dropped call

The CDRs are high-frequency data, normally with low utility except when creating the customer's bill. They are time series data and the volume will increase over time, so they would likely be stored in separate records with a compound key, perhaps "bucketing" this information into daily buckets as described in Chapter 6. Quite often this information will be streamed into the database.

When the call drops, the CDRs would show abnormal call termination. This information could be used to trigger a business process to see if this was a rare occurrence or something more systemic (and hence irritating) to the user. The historical CDRs could be consulted to see how many calls have been dropped in the last week. If they are over a certain threshold, the customer's satisfaction rating could be automatically adjusted on the main customer record. Remedial action could also be taken, such as an email or message sent to the user apologizing for the disruptions and offering a discount or credit based on the frequency. This sort of remedial action, which tries to maintain a holistic view of the customer, can certainly help maintain good customer relationships.

Fraud Detection

Fraud detection typically relies on the comparison of an inbound event to established patterns to which past events have conformed. For example, credit card fraud detection has an inbound event of a credit card swipe (either physical or virtual) and is compared to other credit card swipes from the same user. Typically, comparisons will also be done for the same credit card swipe to use patterns from the same merchant and the same terminal to try to identify merchant fraud or a terminal that has been hacked and is behaving differently from other terminals.

There are many approaches to solving fraud detection. Some use AI techniques and similarity searches to find how similar this transaction is to historical transactions known to be good by the same user. Other approaches use graph techniques to work out patterns between recent transactions. For example, if a credit card has paid for a taxi, a hotel, and a meal in New York and shortly after pays for a dinner in Paris, the latter charge is likely to be fraudulent. However, if the taxi, hotel, and meal were also in Paris, the same charge is much more likely to be genuine.

Irrespective of the approach to solving fraud detection, there is one invariant: the more data you can analyze in the same time period, the better the result. One common approach to this is to use Aerospike to load significant amounts of data in parallel.

There are several different data models that work for fraud detection, depending on the type of algorithm used to detect fraud. These data models range from simple decision trees to complex AI solutions.

Brute Force

Brute force algorithms rely on Aerospike loading significant volumes of data and running a rules engine or AI model across the entirety of this data. In this case, the data being loaded just needs to be the raw transaction data, which can be done using data models similar to those shown in Chapter 6. As a reminder, Figure 10-4 shows that data model.

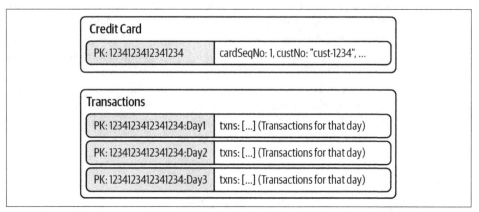

Figure 10-4. Credit card model from Chapter 6 grouping transactions per day

In this case the Aerospike data model is optimized to return the transactions for a specific data range. The keys of the records are computed in code, taking the current date and working out the keys of the records by a simple algorithm so that the transaction records are stored bucketed into one record per customer per day. Once the keys have been computed, a simple batch get can return all the desired records in parallel.

Decision Trees or Neural Networks

While decision trees and neural networks are very different algorithms, they effectively process data in the same way. Decision trees are tree-like structures used to make decisions based on a hierarchical set of decision rules. Decisions at one node based on a set of features or variables in the data set guide the algorithm to the next node. This subsequent node then uses a typically smaller subset of data to further classify the data as fraudulent or valid, and the process is repeated until a decision is reached. Only one record is needed at a time as the required data for the next node is unknown until the next node has been determined. Figure 10-5 shows a diagrammatic comparison of decision trees and neural networks.

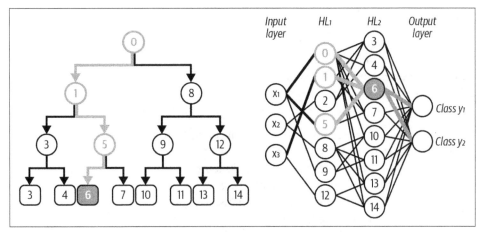

Figure 10-5. A comparison of a decision tree and neural network

In contrast, neural networks are a type of artificial intelligence modeled after the structure of the human brain. A network of nodes is constructed with each node connected to several other nodes, with each connection having a weight to determine the strength of the connection. Once the neural network has been established, the weights are adjusted to try to minimize the error between the expected results and the actual results.

When applying a neural network to a fraud detection problem, it is also normal to load one record at a time, apply the weights of the node, and then, based on the results of this weighting, determine which node to traverse to next.

In both cases, records from the database need to be loaded sequentially, with some computation applied to each node before the next record is loaded. This means that parallelization is not possible. The latency of each individual transaction must be small enough that the sum of all the transactions fits within the SLA for the fraud detection window while leaving time to run the actual fraud detection algorithm.

The SLA for giving a "fraudulent" or "valid" decision varies based on the provider, but they typically range from 120 ms up to about 750 ms. The more data that can be loaded in that time, and the more time left over after the data has been loaded for the fraud detection algorithm to run, the better the result.

Aerospike has proven to be excellent in this domain with some very large online electronic payment providers using Aerospike as the database for their neural network–based fraud detection solutions. The consistently low latency of Aerospike allows hundreds of sequential lookups with plenty of time for the fraud detection algorithm within their fraud detection windows.

Vectors

Vector databases and their semantic search capabilities are becoming well known in the industry. The ability to do searches over large vector spaces for items that are "close to" a representative vector is proving useful in many verticals. Vectors are typically large cardinality arrays of floating-point numbers, and a vectorization algorithm is applied to turn a business object, such as a transaction, into these vectors.

For example, consider a fraud detection scenario utilizing vectors representing transactions stored in a vector database. Some of the dimensions of the vector might include transaction attributes like amount, whether the card was physically present, location of the transaction, type of item being purchased, and so on. The vectors in the database represent a history of transactions, many of which are valid and some of which were determined to be fraudulent.

When a new transaction arrives, it is passed through the same vectorization algorithm to turn it into a vector. Then, the semantic search capabilities of the vector database are invoked to determine the closest set of vectors to this vector, typically using something like a cosine similarity engine. If all the closest vectors to this vector are known to be encoded from fraudulent transactions, it is likely that this transaction is fraudulent too.

While an in-depth discussion of vector databases is beyond the scope of this book, they do form a powerful way of determining fraud, and typically form part of an AI infrastructure. Aerospike can work well as a vector database. Some companies are using Aerospike for fraud prevention and applying AI models on top of Aerospike.

Summary

Aerospike is an excellent database for storing disparate data models for applications that require high scale and low latency. These applications cover a variety of use cases and industry verticals, and the selection presented in this chapter is just a small sample of use cases where Aerospike excels.

Over the course of this book, you should have gained a foundational understanding of the specialized power and scale of Aerospike, as well as a fair understanding of the kinds of challenges it is ideal for. You should now be able to install and operate Aerospike, have a basic understanding of the best ways to model data for it, know how to configure and monitor its health, and have a ground-level knowledge of how it is architected.

We hope this book has given you the knowledge you need to understand which use cases in your company have the kind of low-latency, high-scale requirements that Aerospike is made for. And that it will give you the tools you need to dive in and begin using Aerospike to solve them.

Index

troubleshooting guide, 161
tuning migrations, 158
double data type, 34
durable deletes, 42
dynamic configuration, 131-133
asinfo tool, 133-136
memory-size parameter example, 134

E

Enterprise Edition (see Aerospike Enterprise Edition)
errors
console log entries missing, 127
ignoring errors, 64
eventual consistency, 3
examples of Aerospike in use
Customer 360, 184-187
about, 184
data model, 185
fraud detection, 187-190
about, 187
brute force, 188
decision trees or neural networks, 188
vectors, 190
user profile store, 179-184
about, 179
data model, 180-182
expiry of elements, 182-184
exception thrown when dividing by zero, 64
exists function, 43
Exp class filter expressions, 60
expiration of map entries, 120-122
expiration value for time-to-live, 35
reading a record, 39
ExpOperation class, 63
exporters
node exporter, 162
Prometheus web requests, 152
Aerospike exporter, 152
expressions, 60-65
about, 60
ExpOperation class, 63
filter expressions, 60
multiple predicate queries with secondary indexes, 72
read expressions, 62-65
trilean logic, 61
true, false, unknown, 61

F

fabric of data exchange via port 3001, 14
aerospike.conf specifications, 128
Fast Restart of daemon in Enterprise, 131
filter expressions, 60
flash storage optimization, 4-6
copy-on-write mechanism, 6
massively parallel access, 6
storage architectures supported, 4
submillisecond latency, 83
total cost of ownership lower, 83
fraud detection
Aerospike use case, 187-190
about, 187
brute force, 188
decision trees or neural networks, 188
vectors, 190
PayPal fraud detection, 166

G

GB (gibibytes), 129
generation counter of record, 39
geographically distributed databases
about replication, 165-167
asynchronous replication system, 168-176
about, 168
active-active topologies, 170
active-passive topologies, 169
convergence, 173
mesh topology, 171
non-Aerospike destinations, 174
ordering of updates having limitations, 175
read/write latencies extremely low, 166
rewind, 173
shipping strategy, 171
star topology, 170, 171
multisite clustering, 167
local data-center for reads, 167
master node written to, 167
scenario of one site unavailable, 168
rack awareness, 94-95, 167
synchronous active-active system, 95, 167
payment settlement example, 166
geoJSON data type, 34
get method, 38-40
associated objects, 112
external ID resolution, 116-118
batch operations, 44

expiration of record, 39
generation of record, 39
Policy, 27, 38
primary key, 26
return value
    INVERTED, 58
    operate() command, 50, 58
GiB (gibibytes), 129
gibibytes instead of gigabytes, 129
Grafana for dashboarding Prometheus, 151

H

hash (#) for comments in aerospike.conf, 123
health score, 82
heartbeat messages between nodes, 80
    cluster self-management, 79
    configuration in aerospike.conf, 128
    port 3002 for heartbeats, 14
help for aql command, 142
    aql -? for help with shell, 142
help for asadm, 70, 137
help system for AeroLab, 17, 20
hist.c logging histograms, 146
histograms utility asloglatency, 145-147
HMA (see Hybrid Memory Architecture)
hotspots avoided
    colocating indexes and data, 8
    shared-nothing architecture, 6
Hybrid Memory Architecture™ (HMA), 83-85
    about, 83
        standard filesystem-based versus, 83
    indexes in memory, 4, 83, 130
    key-value read efficiency, 118
    storage architectures supported, 4
HyperLogLog data type, 34

I

ID resolution of external IDs, 116-118
    very small object problem, 118-120
ID storage, 114-116
ignoring errors, 64
in-place updates replaced by copy-on-writes, 6
incremental backups, 145
info command of asadm, 137
    Aerospike exporter, 154
    info protocol
        aerospike.conf, 129
    principal node identification, 162
installation of AeroLab, 17

installation of Aerospike
    about, 11
    Aerospike database, 14
    deployments via AeroLab, 16
    Linux systems, 15
        Aerospike running natively, 11, 15
        installed as a service, 16
    Macintosh systems, 12-15
        Aerospike tools running locally, 15
    Windows systems, 12-15
        Aerospike tools running in containers, 15
installation of Aerospike exporter, 152
integer data type, 34
IP addresses in network context of aerospike.conf, 127

J

Java
    ... (varargs operator), 48
        end of each call, 59
    basic operations
        batch operations, 44
        create, 36-38
        delete, 42
        read, 39-40
        touch to extend TTL, 43
        updates, 41
        upsert behavior, 41
        WritePolicy expiration, 35
    client download page, 24
    data types, 33
    latency tracking metrics, 149
    ordered list for sorted map range of keys, 107
    Record class used, 27
    simple first application, 23-27
        about Python and Java clients, 23
        connection to database, 24-26
        data inserted and retrieved, 26
    TreeMap for ordered Map, 106
jemalloc memory allocator library, 86
joins not supported, 112
journalctl command
    cluster and noninformational messages, 162
    console logs, 126

K

Keys, 26

quorums, 89

R

rack awareness, 94-95
    multisite clustering basis, 94, 167
RDBMS versus Aerospike, 20-23, 97
    joins not supported, 112
read
    associated objects, 112
        key-value read efficiency, 118
    backups reading records, 143
    batch read, 44, 65
        cautions, 65
    concurrent read access, 86
    get method, 38-40
        associated objects, 112
        batch operations, 44
        expiration of record, 39
        external ID resolution, 116-118
        generation of record, 39
        Java code for read, 39-40
        Policy, 38
        primary key, 26
        Python code for read, 39-40
        return value for operate() command, 58
        return value INVERTED, 58
    latencies, 166
        local data-center for reads, 167
    read expressions, 62-65
real-time bidding audience segmentation, 180
records
    Aerospike Quick Look, 27-30
    aggregating subobjects into one record,
        100-106
    automatic cascade on deletion not sup-
        ported, 99
    BatchRecords, 69
    copy on write, 102
    CRUD operations (see CRUD (create, read,
        update, delete))
    data model of Aerospike, 21
        sets, 21
    data types, 33
    external ID resolution, 116-118
        very small object problem, 118-120
    generation of record, 39
    merging many small into one big, 118
    metadata and data components, 61
        last ship time (LST), 171

last update time (LUT), 171
primary key not stored, 114
Record class used, 27
RecordSet returned from queries, 71
    close when finished, 72
secondary indexes, 69-71
simple first application, 23-27
    about Python and Java clients, 23
    connection to database, 24-26
    data inserted and retrieved, 26
time-to-live (TTL), 35
    touching a record to update, 43
upsert record modification, 27
    updates, 41
zombie records, 160
relational database management system versus
    Aerospike, 20-23, 97
    joins not supported, 112
relationships
    associating objects in data modeling,
        110-116
        external ID resolution, 116-118
        reading related objects, 112
        storing IDs, 114-116
        updating relationships, 111
    map between key and value, 34
    partition map of partitions to nodes, 8, 82
replication
    about geographically distributed databases,
        165-167
    asynchronous replication system, 168-176
        about, 168
        active-active topologies, 170
        active-passive topologies, 169
        convergence, 173
        mesh topology, 171
        non-Aerospike destinations, 174
        ordering of updates having limitations,
        175
        read/write latencies extremely low, 166
        rewind, 173
        shipping strategy, 171
        star topology, 170, 171
    multisite clustering, 167
        local data-center for reads, 167
        master node written to, 167
        scenario of one site unavailable, 168
    rack awareness, 94-95, 167
    synchronous active-active system, 95, 167

About the Authors

Dr. V. Srinivasan is the CTO and Founder of Aerospike. When it comes to databases, he is one of the recognized pioneers of Silicon Valley. Srini has two decades of experience in designing, developing, and operating highly scalable infrastructures. He also has over a dozen patents in database, web, mobile, and distributed systems technologies. Srini cofounded Aerospike to solve the scaling problems he experienced with Oracle databases while he was Senior Director of Engineering at Yahoo.

Tim Faulkes is an enterprise application architect with over 20 years of global experience in delivering technical solutions to business problems at an enterprise level. His specialties include application architecture and design, technical team leadership, mentoring and educating developers, and liaising between business and technical teams to ensure high-value solutions are delivered in a timely and effective manner. Tim is currently the Chief Developer Advocate at Aerospike.

Albert Autin is the Lead Database Reliability Engineer at The Trade Desk. His current responsibilities include managing the data ingestion team, advising and optimizing on data structures and access patterns in the Aerospike ecosystem, and creating and testing new capacity planning methods. Albert also works with business and project leadership to plan and prioritize short- and long-term goals. He has over a decade of experience working with the Aerospike database.

Paige Roberts has worked for over 25 years as an engineer, trainer, support technician, technical writer, product marketer, product manager, and a consultant all in the data management and analytics field. While possibly a little fuzzy on what she wants to do when she grows up, she's always passionate about data technology. Over the years, at companies like Data Junction, Pervasive, the Bloor Group, Hortonworks, Syncsort, Vertica, and thatDot, she continues to promote greater understanding of distributed data processing, data engineering architectures, and accelerating the process of extracting usefulness from data. For O'Reilly, she also coauthored *Accelerate Machine Learning with a Unified Analytics Architecture* and contributed to *97 Things Every Data Engineer Should Know*. Her goal is to help bridge the gap between brilliant technical minds and practical business outcomes.

Colophon

The animal on the cover of *Aerospike: Up and Running* is a European hedgehog (*Erinaceus europaeus*). Also known as the common hedgehog, this spiny mammal can be found in the United Kingdom and all throughout Europe, from Italy to Scandinavia.

European hedgehogs are widely known for the brown and white spines that cover their small, round bodies. Adult hedgehogs have about five to seven thousand spines, which they use to protect themselves against predators. When threatened, hedgehogs raise their spines in a criss-cross pattern as they curl into a ball, shielding their soft white bellies from attacks. In terms of size, hedgehogs are short and small, ranging from 6 to 12 inches long (excluding their tails, which are roughly 1 to 2 inches long) and can weigh up to 4.5 pounds.

Hedgehogs like to live in field edges and hedgerows; throughout the UK, they can also be found in suburban gardens and parks. They are nocturnal animals and usually feast on insects, such as earthworms, ants, and crickets, and sometimes snails and slugs. Although they are not considered an endangered species, their population is on the decline in the UK due to habitation loss.

Many of the animals on O'Reilly covers are endangered; all of them are important to the world.

The cover illustration is by Jose Marzan, based on an antique line engraving from *Brehms Thierleben*. The series design is by Edie Freedman, Ellie Volckhausen, and Karen Montgomery. The cover fonts are Gilroy Semibold and Guardian Sans. The text font is Adobe Minion Pro; the heading font is Adobe Myriad Condensed; and the code font is Dalton Maag's Ubuntu Mono.

O'REILLY®

Learn from experts.
Become one yourself.

Books | Live online courses
Instant answers | Virtual events
Videos | Interactive learning

Get started at oreilly.com.

Printed in the USA
CPSIA information can be obtained
at www.ICGtesting.com
JSHW061409091124
73248JS00008B/235

9 781098 155605